EYES OF
INTEGRITY

XXXchurch.com resource

EYES OF INTEGRITY

THE PORN PANDEMIC
AND HOW IT AFFECTS YOU

CRAIG GROSS

WITH JASON HARPER

BakerBooks
a division of Baker Publishing Group
Grand Rapids, Michigan

© 2010 by Craig Gross

Published by Baker Books
a division of Baker Publishing Group
P.O. Box 6287, Grand Rapids, MI 49516-6287
www.bakerbooks.com

Printed in the United States of America

Library of Congress Cataloging-in-Publication Data
Gross, Craig, 1975–
    Eyes of integrity : the porn pandemic and how it affects you / Craig Gross with Jason Harper.
        p. cm.
    Includes bibliographical references (p.   ).
    ISBN 978-0-8010-7205-5 (pbk.)
    1. Pornography—Religious aspects—Christianity. 2. Christian life. I. Harper, Jason, 1971– II. Title.
BV4597.6.G76 2010
241′.667—dc22   2010014459

Craig Gross is represented by Wheelhouse Literary Group, 1007 Loxley Drive, Nashville, TN 37211.

To protect the privacy of those whose stories are shared by the authors, some names and details have been changed.

In keeping with biblical principles of creation stewardship, Baker Publishing Group advocates the responsible use of our natural resources. As a member of the Green Press Initiative, our company uses recycled paper when possible. The text paper of this book is comprised of 30% post-consumer waste.

10   11   12   13   14   15   16   7   6   5   4   3   2   1

This book is dedicated to my friend Steve Glisan. Thank you for your passion, love, and care for the people you served in this ministry. I miss you and wish I could have let you know I was here for you.

Steve, you were a great man of God! You are greatly missed.

Contents

Preface

It was the mid-nineties. I was a youth pastor in Southern California and was sitting in my office hearing about one of my students—we'll call him Tommy—and a recent blowout he'd had with lust.

It had to do with this new thing, this invention called the internet. More and more of my students were coming to me with stories about satisfying their lust through this latest source. In years past if someone wanted porn, they had to work for it, trekking, under cloak of night, to a seedy neighborhood. I imagine a man sneaking into the local quick stop to buy a *Hustler*, wearing a trench coat and fedora pulled down to his eyebrows.

But with the launch of the internet in the early nineties, porn was on a new kind of page. Instead of buying a magazine with a limited number of pictures, the internet offered an endless supply, accessible to everyone with a computer and an internet connection. With a few clicks and some refined searching, a young user—like the student in my office—could find just about any type of porn he wanted and then some.

Though I had been dreading this meeting with Tommy and his mother, Sherry, I knew we needed to talk. I could tell when he called me a few days ago, adamant about seeing me as soon as possible, something was wrong.

So on the day of our appointment, Tommy stumbled into my office with a dazed look on his face and an angry mom in his wake.

Tears running down her cheeks, Sherry went from angry to sad to hopeless as she told me, her voice barely above a whisper, about walking into her home office. She found Tommy glued to the computer screen, so entranced by the porn site in front of him that he was oblivious to her being there.

Now in my office Tommy felt ashamed and awkward as his mother and I quizzed him on his activity. Our thirty-minute appointment turned into a two-hour session as the three of us tried to uncover the strong seduction of internet porn in Tommy's life.

When our meeting was over and Tommy and Sherry had left, I was the one in a helpless daze. I hardly knew what the internet was, much less the ways it was destroying this young man. I didn't know what to say to this kid or to any of the other kids who were now suddenly struggling with this new phenomenon. I was at a loss.

Days passed and I still hadn't given Tommy a practical plan or any helpful advice. I just didn't know where to start. I probably told him to read his Bible more, pray consistently, and come to the next midweek service—all the standard answers when you don't know what to say. Hardly the complete answer I would give him if he came to my office today.

I tell this story for a reason. That encounter with Tommy and his mother was the first time I realized how destructive porn is—the way it consumes and corrupts the hearts and minds of good people whom we think should know better.

Over the next couple years, more and more of my students became entangled in the web of pornography, and I kept searching for a way to help them. I was overwhelmed by the sheer number of lives that porn left broken. It was taking people farther than they ever thought they would go and influencing them to do things they never thought they would do.

Porn had become a pandemic.

A *pandemic* is an epidemic of an infectious disease that spreads through populations across a large region. Often polls produce inflated numbers and statistics can embellish a problem, but with porn, I think reality is much worse than the numbers indicate. I mean, who wants to admit in a survey to having a problem with porn?

But help is available.

No addict ever started off saying, "I hope I become an addict someday." Addiction comes after a lot of bad choices and continues as long as the bad choices are made. If we could somehow help prevent the bad choices, we could then help overcome the addiction.

After talking with a computer programming friend of mine, we came up with the concept of an accountability software program. In its earliest version the idea was simple. Load the software onto the computer and then go about your online business. The program would instruct users to enlist a friend as an accountability partner. Then every two or four weeks (depending on the frequency you chose), a list of any questionable websites you visited would be sent to your accountability partner. Now you had someone looking over your shoulder as you surfed the web; hopefully that knowledge would keep you from getting sucked into the vortex of porn. We named it X3watch and gave it away to anyone who wanted it.

And that was the beginning of what I do today. My friend and I strategized and decided to roll out a website to help people who needed it the most: the Las Vegas Adult Video Convention. Dreaming outside the box, we purchased a booth at the Adult Video Trade Show and branded ourselves "XXX-church: The #1 Christian Porn Site."

You may wonder where that name originated. We mixed the seedy (XXX) with the sacred (church) to make this statement: the church can have an impact on the lives of those who are being destroyed by pornography addiction.

We had a unique approach to ministry, so we generated quite a few critics but even more converts. We pressed forward, offering spiritual solutions to porn addiction on our website and appearing every January in Vegas with a vision not only to give software away to porn addicts but also to help those in the adult industry escape if they wanted to.

That was eight years ago at the time of this writing, and during those eight years we've heard so many stories of hope and struggle. Nearly a million people have downloaded the free X3watch software (available at XXXchurch.com), while our website continues to have more than a million hits per month. We've relocated our ministry from Southern California to Las Vegas and do outreach on the notorious Vegas Strip, offering the many adult industry workers in the city a place to escape.

Churches around the world continue to call us, asking if we can train and teach their congregations about ways to deal with the porn issue. We've launched spin-off ministries, and we are constantly being challenged to stay current on the buzz and blitz of an ever-changing online world.

This book is intended to be a satellite image of the vast problem before us and an alarm to let people know how deadly this vice can be. We also hope it will be a helping hand. If you're already caught in the grip of porn, this book will help you navigate your way to freedom. We're committed to equipping churches and individuals to overcome the power of porn.

I encourage you to first read this book as one who seeks, with God's help, never to be trapped by the net of porn. Second, keep it on hand to give away when someone you love needs help. We have learned over the years that porn has long fingers that reach everyone. If it hasn't affected you directly, it has affected or will affect someone close to you.

God's grace and Jesus's redemptive work on the cross are stronger than the grip of porn. It's up to you to make the right choices.

Guarded but hopeful,
Craig Gross

HOW BAD IS IT?

ONE

Pornified World

The Development
of a Massive Societal Sickness

I remember seeing porn as a kid at my Christian school one day during track when some of my teammates had a magazine. I got a small glimpse but not enough to really know what I was looking at. Shortly after that preliminary exposure, I went to my friend Sean's house. He lived just down the road, and most days after school I stopped in. His parents were rarely there, and they thought it a rite of passage for seventh-grade boys to gratify and explore their lust with a *Playboy*. I had heard of *Playboy* before but I had never seen one . . . until that day at Sean's.

Out of the blue Sean said, "I want to show you something."

We went to the backyard and into his mom's garden. He held this magazine out to me and asked if I wanted to see it. To this day, I can remember the way my heart reverberated through my chest as my curiosity got the best of me and I accepted his offer. I flipped to the first page.

Sean snatched the magazine back, simultaneously opening it to the mythical centerfold, its crinkled pages unfolding in slow motion and introducing my innocent twelve-year-old mind to something new, thrilling, and deeply disconcerting.

Trying to appear as cool as the more experienced Sean, I willed my cheeks to stop blushing. The image seared itself in my mind, and to this day, more than twenty-five years later, I can still recall it.

After a few minutes we put the magazine away and I got ready to leave. I went into the house to grab my backpack and ran into Sean's mother, who was standing in the living room. As I walked past her, the images I'd just seen danced in my mind, and I couldn't even speak to her.

That night I lay in bed awake, still pondering what I'd experienced. I had been brought up around the church and had been told to respect women. Though my adolescent curiosity had stoked past searches of my house for visual contraband, the worst I had ever found was a copy of *National Geographic*.

But now new images flashed again and again through my mind, and from that afternoon on, the innocence of my elementary years was gone. I felt different—in a way older, in another way dirty. The way that centerfold model had been posing didn't seem healthy, normal, or natural. I tried to puzzle out the identity of the man with her. Was that her husband? And who was the *other* person, and what was making her face contort that way? On that one afternoon, a series of unanswered questions surfaced: Where did Sean get that magazine? Did he steal it? Was it a gift? There's no way a twelve-year-old kid could walk up to a counter in a store and buy it. Could I get one? Did *every* kid have one? Had every kid seen what I'd seen? Was it normal for a kid my age to see something like that?

I had been introduced to the world of porn. The small spark of my curiosity was now a raging fire—one that, over time and with God's help, I would learn to control.

Often porn begins as a cunning siren call, but it can quickly turn into a ferocious monster. So many people have had their lives destroyed, their families destroyed, their jobs destroyed because they were curious. Little did they know that curiosity is almost always the first step to all-out addiction. Sometimes that first step is well intentioned. I know several Christian men who have been lured into the world of porn because they wanted to be educated about the dangers lurking on the internet.

It's natural to be curious; after all, God made us sexual beings. But because porn is now so easy to obtain, most of us need tough safeguards in place to keep us from becoming the proverbial cat, killed by our own curiosity.

The Evolving World of Porn

Sex is often referred to as "the world's oldest profession," and as long as it has been around, people have wanted to look at it. While it's been a part of society from the beginning, its social, psychological, and economic impact throughout history is tough to determine.

In 1969 President Lyndon Johnson and the U.S. Congress funded an investigation into the issue called "The President's

Commission on Obscenity and Pornography," which laid the groundwork for what we define today as porn.

Basically the commission decided that porn was benign, estimating only about 10 million dollars' worth of porn in the United States at the time. Essentially they said porn wasn't a threat, that it was okay, as long as you kept it away from kids, a finding that fit in well with the free-thinking sexual "revolution" occurring at the time.[1] Shortly after this ruling, in 1972, the X-rated and iconographic porn film *Deep Throat* appeared in theaters, its depictions of hardcore sex causing a stir on both sides of the political spectrum.

Film critic Roger Ebert writes:

> The modern era of skin flicks began in 1960 with Russ Meyer's *The Immoral Mr. Teas*, which inspired Meyer and others to make a decade of films featuring nudity but no explicit sex. Then a Supreme Court ruling seemed to permit the hardcore stuff, and *Deep Throat* was the first film to take it to a mass audience. . . . [People] lined up for [it] and talked cheerfully to news cameras about wanting to see it because, well, everybody else seemed to be going.[2]

It's difficult to get an accurate assessment of the money *Deep Throat* made at the box office, but its cultural impact is undeniable. The movie made porn mainstream, packing out theaters with people beyond the trench coat brigade. It was considered a "date" movie and paved the way for more of the same. Then came the '80s and the creation of home video, then the DVD, then the internet.

Today pornography is a 57-billion-dollar, worldwide industry, making more than the combined revenues of all the professional football, baseball, and basketball teams in America. Porn revenue in the United States (12 billion dollars) exceeds the combined revenues of ABC, CBS, and NBC (6.2 billion dollars), and, disgustingly enough, child pornography alone generates 3 billion dollars annually. In 2005 national online data polling estimated that one out of every ten websites is pornographic. Twenty percent of men admitted to looking at online porn while at work, while far more admit to using it in the privacy of their homes.

Today pornography is a 57-billion-dollar, worldwide industry, making more than the combined revenues of all the professional football, baseball, and basketball teams in America.

Things have definitely changed. Forget *National Geographic* or sitting in a garden—today's twelve-year-olds have only to browse the internet to find a lot more than a single centerfold. And because the kids in the house are the ones teaching Mom and Dad how to use the computer, the kids—boys and girls alike—are usually savvy enough to navigate around any filter their parents might put on the computer. Plus, carrying thousands of images on a single CD or flash drive makes flying under the radar easy.

According to a Wharton study:

> The common wisdom is that pornographic material is the dirty secret of the Internet, accounting for vast amounts of traffic and enormous revenues. Jupiter Media Metrix, a company

which tracks Internet usage, found that 30 million different users visited adult sites in March, accounting for 33.8 percent of all people who used the world wide web, according to media development coordinator Kumar Rao.[3]

One study reported that 72 percent of those who dabble in porn are men and 28 percent are women. This study also found that more than 220 million dollars was spent at fee-based sites in 2001, up from 148 million dollars in 1999. By 2005 the number was up to an estimated 320 million dollars.[4] Our world is becoming increasingly more pornified, and the profits prove it.

Consider porn on a per-second basis. Every second 3,076 dollars is being spent on pornography, 28,258 internet viewers are viewing pornography, and 372 internet users are typing adult search terms into search engines, and every 39 minutes, a new pornographic video is made in the United States.[5]

The infiltration of porn into homes across America has increased exponentially even over the last ten years. According to a PBS *Frontline* story called "American Porn," the majority of male internet users get the internet in their homes to have easy access to porn.[6] *Frontline* also reported that the greatest single catalyst encouraging men to use online porn was the infamous "sex tape" featuring rock drummer Tommy Lee and his Playboy Playmate wife Pamela Anderson. Once it was made available online, internet subscriptions skyrocketed.

Then men were able to use the web to explore their own sexual desires with no waiting, no worries, and no witnesses. They have bought into it hook, line, and sinker, and the porn industry has the receipts to prove it.

Such easily accessed porn has increased the number of sex addicts. Teachers, doctors, clergy, athletes, lawyers, blue-collar workers—you name it—porn does not play favorites.

Pornified World

In our ministry we've reached out not just to addicts but also to those who produce or star in porn, and in our conversations we've learned that many of them do not feel they are to blame for the problem porn has become. To them, it is simple supply-and-demand economics: if the demand is there for porn, they have a right to produce it. Porn is a business—a highly profitable one. General Motors, AOL, Time Warner, and Marriott are just a few of the megacorporations that enjoy profits from funneling adult movies into American homes and hotel rooms.

While some companies increase profits by producing porn, other companies have struck gold by distributing it.

While some companies increase profits by producing porn, other companies have struck gold by distributing it. Whether through ISPs, server space, or web hosting, hundreds of major companies are taking a slice of the pie. *Frontline* reported it is rare for financial business reports to explain the depths of these companies' involvement in porn and their resulting financial gain.

Familiarity breeds desensitization, and our culture has definitely become familiar with porn. Consider television. In the 1970s, shows such as *The Love Boat* and *Three's Company* pushed the risqué envelope; today they would be considered tame and harmless sitcoms. Now we have the popular show *The Girls Next Door* glamorizing the lives of *Playboy* models. All the talk about porn, interviews with porn stars, and even a clothing line called "Porn Star" have made porn much less taboo.

Cyberporn reporter Luke Ford "agrees that polite society is embracing porn like never before. 'It's true porn has become chic. Howard Stern, *The Man Show* on Comedy Central feature porn actresses. It's becoming more mainstream in the past five years,' he says."[7]

People entertain forms of visual stimulation that at one time were beyond the pale. Dennis McAlpine, an entertainment industry analyst, stated, "[The porn industry] keep[s] testing the limits to see how far it can get." McAlpine continued, "[The media culture] show[s] one area that becomes accepted; so you go to the next one. And you go to the next one. And things that ten years ago were not permissible now are accepted by society."[8]

The Human Face of a Pandemic: Frank

I met Frank for the first time in a local coffeehouse. He was tall and slender, dressed much more formally than I was. While I was waiting for my latte to cool, we started talking. Quick-witted and very smart, Frank told me how he had used his knowledge of computers to climb the ladder of a local tech company, helping them build secure computer systems and shoring up loose ends within programs to prevent hacking.

Unfortunately, his vocation had also given him insider knowledge of ways to hide things that only experts like him could ever uncover.

He was involved in his church and loved his wife. In our first meetings over coffee, Frank spent hours explaining to me the way porn had subtly infiltrated his home and consumed his life. As a boy and adolescent, he was never intrigued by it, but something changed. He happened on a late-night television show, which led him to the rat wheel of sexual addiction.

His wife had gone to bed early, so Frank began surfing channels through the late-night television lineup. More because of budget than convictions, Frank and his wife had decided to have only basic cable, no movie channels. Some of the guys at work talked about late-night movie channels—Cinemax, for example, or as his friends called it, "Skinamax." Cinemax was one of the first premier channels that featured late-night porn. Frank knew better. No movie channels.

That night, as his eyes began to get heavy, his attention was caught by *The Howard Stern Show*, a televised version of Stern's notoriously raunchy radio program. Noticing a scantily clad woman on the screen, Frank paused, his eyes opened wide, and in an instant he was captivated. Sure, all her private areas had been blurred by the show's producers for airing on television, but Frank's soul was aroused, the lurid seduction pulling at him like a powerful magnet.

Frank watched Stern, shock jock and self-designated "King of All Media," beckon the woman to undress, and she willingly obeyed, disrobing to the cheers of the studio audience.

"At that moment," Frank said, "a fire was lit in me. I wanted to see what the censors had blurred. When the stripper plugged her website, it was over. In the privacy of my home and with my wife asleep, I knew I could log on and see whatever I wanted. My encounter with porn had begun."

Now, three years later, Frank and I meet frequently to discuss healthy ways to stay clear of his unhealthy visual addictions. Still vulnerable, Frank is continually assaulted by a media culture that drove him to sexual overload.

For Frank, the struggle is most intense late at night when his wife is asleep. The moment their heads hit the pillow, Frank often tosses and turns in angst and anxiety while his wife drifts off into slumber, oblivious to his inner turmoil. On nights when he gives in to the temptation, Frank slides out of bed and tiptoes to his office, stepping carefully through the darkened hallway. Though his office is only feet away from his bedroom, once behind his desk, Frank is miles from the intimacy of his bed.

The pornified world we live in sells millions of users that very same lie every day, convincing people that the net of porn is too big, too strong, too wide, and too deep to escape.

The computer boots, each relatively quiet click and whir amplified by his guilty conscience. Describing a particular rendezvous, Frank's voice crackles with regret and guilt. His eyes gloss with tears. "Usually I know exactly where to go to get maximum arousal as quickly as possible."

Within four minutes, Frank logs off—another failure, another check mark on his guilty conscience. He goes back upstairs and slides into bed, his guilt preventing him from getting close to his wife. The experience has been porn, pleasure, and pain.

I wish I could say something that would solve Frank's problem, but I can't make his choices for him. Often he asks, "How did I allow this to infiltrate my house? Why did I not have the strength to say no?"

Frank is not alone. The pornified world we live in sells millions of users that very same lie every day, convincing people that the net of porn is too big, too strong, too wide, and too deep to escape. Hundreds of others log on daily to the "Confessions" page of XXXchurch.com to vent their guilt. Every day we hear from many people whose lives have been reduced to rubble by the porn pandemic.

The statistics and my own experience with XXXchurch.com make one thing very clear—we have a pandemic on our hands and we desperately need to do something about it.

Unfortunately, the problem is not just a secular one; it's infiltrated the church as well.

Pornified Church

How Christians Have Failed to Escape

There are millions of people like Frank—both men and women—in America today. They coach Little League, work in the cubicle next to you, volunteer at school . . . even invite your family over for a barbecue. In fact they're likely the parents of your child's best friend. And they also go to church. Sometimes, they even pastor one.

From the outside, they usually look normal, successful, and even happy. But deep beneath the surface is a dark and illicit drive toward debauchery. They hate it even while they long for it. Their addiction seems to haunt them everywhere and, when given the chance, they will feed it.

For years the faith community as a whole seemed immune to the effects of porn, while many preachers and evangelists railed against the porn industry as being an evil that was second only to the Antichrist. Yet seated in the pews in every church in America are people who add to the pornography demand.

Sunday school teachers, choir members, deacons, board members, and even pastors are becoming addicted.

Most estimates put the number of Christians in the United States at 40 million, and a recent anonymous study done by Promise Keepers discovered that 54 percent of pastors had viewed porn in the previous seven days. If that is the number of *pastors*, how many people in the pews are using too? It's safe to say that some 20 million Christians are using some form of illicit material *every week*.

It's safe to say that some 20 million Christians are using some form of illicit material every week.

The church has become pornified.

Porn has invaded the church, and more than a few still choose to wink at it. A Barna Research Group study released in November 2003 found "four out of five born-again Christians believe pornography to be morally unacceptable. The Bible likens lust to adultery and fornication, both expressly forbidden."[1] That leaves 20 percent of Christians who think porn is okay.

Want more proof of the problem? Here are some staggering numbers about *women* in the church:

- 60 percent of churchgoing females admitted to having significant struggles with lust.
- 40 percent admitted to being involved in sexual sin in the past year.
- 20 percent struggle with looking at pornography on an ongoing basis.[2]

Another survey indicates one out of every six women, including Christians, struggles with an addiction to pornography. That's 17 percent of the population, which, according to a survey by research organization Zogby International, is the number of women who truly believe they can find sexual fulfillment on the internet.[3]

"More than 80 percent of women who have this addiction take it offline," says Marnie Ferree. "Women, far more than men, are likely to act out their behaviors in real life, such as having multiple partners, casual sex, or affairs."[4]

Look into any faith circle and you'll find stories of sensuous and seductive sabotage. From high-profile scandals in the evangelical world to moneymaking, porn-peddling Mormons, I have yet to find a gathering of religious-minded people who are exempt from the porn pandemic. Make no mistake: porn is alive and thriving in the church.

The Neglected Elephant in the Evangelical Room

Just before the summer of 2006, everything was going Ted Haggard's way. He was the lead pastor of New Life Church in Colorado Springs, Colorado, as well as the founder of the Association of Life-Giving Churches. He had been the president of the National Association of Evangelicals (NAE) since 2003. He was the go-to guy for Christianity, the public face of evangelicalism.

But Haggard's public facade crumbled when allegations surfaced about his involvement with drugs and a homosexual relationship with a male prostitute named Mike Jones. Initially Haggard denied even knowing Mike Jones.

In the midst of the madness, trusted and well-known voices from Haggard's evangelical world rallied on his behalf and defended him. As they did, Haggard must have known it was just a matter of time before it backfired and his trusted confidants would be cut off at the knees and overextended, having walked the plank for him.

It was all true. As the media investigated and turned up the facts, Ted Haggard, the family man and pastor, who had used his platform to bark at homosexuals and crusade for family values, acknowledged that he had indeed purchased methamphetamine and had been sexually immoral with Jones.

On Sunday, November 5, 2006, a New Life Church pastor read a letter from Haggard that stated:

> I am so sorry for the circumstances that have caused shame and embarrassment for all of you. . . . The fact is I am guilty of sexual immorality, and I take responsibility for the entire problem. I am a deceiver and a liar. There is a part of my life that is so repulsive and dark that I've been warring against it all of my adult life. . . . The accusations that have been leveled against me are not all true, but enough of them are true that I have been appropriately and lovingly removed from ministry.[5]

Two years later, after tearful appearances on *The Oprah Winfrey Show* and *Larry King Live* and a documentary about his fall, Haggard was caught in another scandal/cover-up. This time, a college student from Haggard's church talked about his night spent in a hotel room with Haggard as he observed the pastor masturbate while watching pornography.[6]

How could this happen? How could a man speak out so vocally against something in public while secretly indulging in the same thing in private? There are many layers to Ted Haggard's fall, but most notable is the psychological phenomenon *reaction formation*. In Sigmund Freud's psychoanalytic theory, reaction formation is a defense mechanism in which anxiety-producing or unacceptable emotions are replaced by their direct opposites.[7] For Haggard, who struggled with homosexuality, reaction formation led to his vehement opposition to homosexuality.

But what does this have to do with a pornified church? The point is that no one is immune, and Haggard is not the first high-profile pastor to fall victim to sexual sin. He won't be the last.

Long seen as crusaders for family values, tight morals, and religious tenacity, the Mormon church has also been impacted by adult entertainment. Marriott Hotel chairman and CEO J. W. "Bill" Marriott Jr., a major contributor to the Mormon church, was recently caught in the middle of a debacle when someone called him on his decrying porn in public while making wads of cash off it via his hotels.

Outside the internet, the hotel industry's on-demand movie service is one of the greatest engines propelling porn's mountainous rise in popularity. Seated at the top of this heap of revenues generated by in-room porn is the Marriott Corporation. The corporate board, headed by Bill Marriott, denounced pornography while quietly pocketing a fortune by offering it in their hotels.

Phil Burress of Ohio's Citizens for Community Values said it best: "Marriott is a major pornographer and even though they may have fought it, everyone on that board is a hypocrite for presenting themselves as family values when their hotels offer 70 different types of hardcore pornography."[8]

While significant theological and doctrinal differences exist between Mormons and evangelicals, they have at least one thing in common—they profess one thing (opposition to porn and the importance of family values, for example), and yet some of their most prominent members do another.

Consider the Haggard fiasco and think about this. Rumors circulated a full year before the story broke that he was dabbling in the homosexual world. Think about the chain of events that must have led up to his fall. We don't know for sure, but it's highly doubtful that he woke up one day and headed to Denver to seek out drugs and sex from a male prostitute. Somewhere along the way he had opened the gateway of his soul to lust and illicit behavior. Maybe it happened when he was a kid. Regardless of when, at one point in his life he opened Pandora's box, releasing into his life the evil of pornography and sexual sin.

Ted Haggard is human and makes mistakes just like the rest of us. But I would guess that, long before his public fall, his conscience had been numbed through porn and this provided the perfect breeding ground for the chaos that ensued.

I sincerely hope he's able to deal with the issues facing him and his family. I hope Bill Marriott puts his money where his mouth is and cleans up the programming in his hotel rooms.

Both of these examples represent so many other people—men and women—who are reeling from the effects of adult entertainment.

Christians Confess

Regardless of age, financial stability, or social status, the people who write to us at XXXchurch and post in the forums, many of them Christians, almost always give the same confession:

porn has given them more pain than they bargained for. Consider this confession from someone we'll call Mark: "Having been raised in a fundamental Baptist church in the early '50s, I was very active in Sunday school, evening worship, and youth group. I even studied to be a minister at two Christian colleges. . . . Through all of my adult life, I have flirted with porn—traveling 75% of the time throughout the U.S., visiting gentlemen's clubs, given to frequent masturbation, and trying to maintain a demanding job and hide my addiction to sex. It has destroyed three marriages and nearly brought me to suicide."

Porn has given them more pain than they bargained for.

Or this one from Don: "Hey, I am Don. I'm ashamed of myself. Every time I click the 'please click if you are over 18' button, I wonder what on earth I am doing here. This is not God's plan for my life! But that does not last long. I soon get into my addiction and I find it hard to press the exit button. I have had this addiction since I was 13 and I have stopped for a period of time. But I found it hard and gave up and it came back. I really need help with this. I don't know who to tell so I came here and I hope you can help me!"

These two heartfelt confessions hardly read like words from guys who are brazen or rooted in hardness toward God. Instead, they sound a lot like a psalm from Scripture: "I know my transgressions, and my sin is always before me. . . . Create in me a pure heart, O God, and renew a steadfast spirit within me" (Ps. 51:3, 10).

Despite his failures as a husband and father, David, the author of Psalm 51, is referred to throughout Scripture as someone who was very special to God. David's penchant to sin is not unusual. Throughout history, people who passionately pursue God and who have a strong grasp of Scripture have failed in the area of sexual integrity. Consider two of the many pastoral confessions we have received at XXXchurch.

Confession from Pastor One

"I'm twenty-five and recently married and interviewing at churches for pastoral positions. I've struggled with porn addiction since I was twelve years old. Through high school and Bible college, I have not been able to get a hold of this. But I desperately want a change for my own sake, my marriage, and for the sake of the congregation that I will serve in ministry. As I read through the other pastors' confessions, I realize that we all struggle exactly in the same way, and knowing that gives me great hope. I always just thought that this issue would go away with the progression of life and maturity, but I learned that it didn't. In fact it got worse. So here I am in my prime years and struggling with an issue that can ruin my ministry, my family, and my own relationship with God. I need help desperately and will do what I need to do before it gets worse. To all you other pastors, I prayed for you as I read your confessions."

Confession from Pastor Two

"I'm a pastor of a small church. I've been keeping an eye on this blog for a while, and I figured it was time to speak up. Quite simply, my life is jacked up. Yes, as you guessed I have a dirty little secret called pornography. I've managed to hide it from my wife, two teenage daughters, and my small church, and I live feeling guilty every day of the week.

"I lead a double life. I'm a full-time pastor but most of the time I just stay alone in my church office, downloading a lot of porn videos off the internet, and I'm just completely unable to stop it. I even bought an extra hard drive just to keep those videos and it's already getting full.

"The most painful moment in my life is when my daughters give me a hug and tell me they love me and they think I'm the greatest guy in the whole world. That hurts, but it's still better than having two angry daughters cursing me for my porn addiction.

"My wife and I haven't been intimate for years now because I just don't feel like that with her anymore. She doesn't do all the naughty stuff like those girls in video clips, and she isn't as physically attractive as those young girls. Fortunately, she isn't interested in sex all that much, so she seems to think it's kind of cool that I'm not needy in that sense.

"So, guys, stay away from porn at all costs!

"If you can't, at least do a good job hiding it from your family and church. It's better to do that than making them go through hell. In my case, I pretty much gave up on myself. I simply pray that God will use my preaching independent of my personal struggles so more people would come and support my church. The Gospel must move forward regardless of my personal issues. That's what matters."

Sadly, this second confession, as frustrating and distressing as it is, eerily reflects the logic of many porn users, which is why I included it here. Let's look at it in detail: "I just stay alone in my church office, downloading a lot of porn videos off the internet, and *I'm just completely unable to stop it*."

I believe he's sincere in his desire, but "I'm just completely unable to stop" is a statement of self-deception. Many people say they are unable to stop when their actual problem is completely different: they do not really *want* to stop. In reality it is possible to stop, but not without God's help and a supportive community. If this pastor was being honest with himself, he would say, "I am unable to stop because I am not willing to deal with the consequences of my actions."

Many people say they are unable to stop when their actual problem is completely different: they do not really want to stop.

"My daughters give me a hug and tell me they love me and they think I'm the greatest guy in the whole world. That hurts, *but it's still better than having two angry daughters cursing me for my porn addiction*." His daughters express love that is genuine, but Dad undermines the power of that love by not receiving it with truth and purity. Instead, he wants to keep up his lie forever and not get caught.

This pastor has, like hundreds of other pastors addicted to porn, made a huge and arrogant error in judgment, betting he won't make a wrong step. But all it takes is one mishap and his world will crumble. Then his loving daughters will have to deal with the sudden realization that their formerly great dad had been lying to them for years.

A father's *betrayal* always hurts more than a father's *failure*. Yes, if this pastor came clean, it would hurt his family and break a lot of trust. It would take time to rebuild his family and his ministry, but his vulnerability would carry him to a higher level of authentic wholeness that would speed the healing.

On the other hand, should his wife, kids, and congregation find out the hard way—stumbling into his office while he's using, checking out that hard drive, noticing a porn purchase on a receipt—the damage would likely be irreparable. This pastor is making a colossal error, but his faulty logic and judgment are common among addicts.

"My wife and I haven't been intimate for years now because I just don't feel like that with her anymore. *She doesn't do all the naughty stuff like those girls in the video clips, and she isn't as physically attractive as those young girls.*" This is the pinnacle of the porn problem. People who have actively used porn inevitably compare their online fantasy to their real-world relationship, and in such comparisons, reality will always lose out, because *porn is not reality.*

The use of porn alters brain chemicals, and in this pastor's case these chemicals attached sexual arousal to the images embedded in his computer screen. Like a well-trained Pavlovian dog, his mind and sexual triggers have been altered and now only react under pornographic stimuli. Fantasy has become the anchor of his arousal.

Note also his alarming use of the words "young girls." Granted, he doesn't state his own age or how old the "young girls" are. However, whenever I see or hear someone referencing young girls in the context of porn use, I get protective. I'm not suggesting he's breaking the law, but we at XXXchurch have had to drop more than a few people off at a prison gate to begin serving time after they were convicted on child porn charges. Porn keeps twisting you until you break.

"Stay away from porn at all costs! *If you can't, at least do a good job hiding it from your family and church.* It's better to do that than making them go through hell." Here he offers some advice: stay away from porn at all costs. Unfortunately, this very good advice is undercut by the reality of his deception—but if you can't, hide it well. *What?!* Hiding issues in any area of life is complete sabotage—not to mention stupid. The New Testament is clear that all unconfessed failures will be shouted from the rooftops (John 3:19–21; Eph. 5:8–14; 1 Cor. 4:5; and 1 John 1:8–10 come to mind). Nothing will remain hidden.

His selfish and cowardly attitude is not uncommon among porn addicts, though. People hide their failures, telling themselves it's because they want to spare those who are close to them. They decide wrongly it's best to keep their addiction hidden.

Porn keeps twisting you until you break.

"I simply pray that God will use my preaching independent of my personal struggles *so more people would come and support my church.*" At this point in his life, church growth should be the least of his concerns. But here's the thing—he may well receive financial support. Many times people have had short-term success even though they were living a life that was in complete shambles. Think Jim Bakker, Jimmy Swaggart, Ted Haggard, and so on.

My fear for this pastor, apart from the obvious, is that he will see some limited effectiveness and maybe even some success in his ministry. My fear is that he'll think God has winked at his sin or allowed him to continue for the sake of "ministry." Such a mind-set would reek of flagrant pride and arrogance; and yet it is the prayer of this pastor's heart. He wants God to display his power in ministry but not in this pastor's addiction—selfishness to the extreme.

I wish this confession were an isolated incident, but I can tell you from experience it isn't. We see confessions like these from pastors and other Christians every day. Christians, pastors, CEOs, soccer moms—no one is outside the reach of porn's grip. All are susceptible, and all need to be cautious in their daily activities to avoid being caught up in porn.

Christians in the Industry

The first time I talked to Pete, I was concerned he was suicidal. He sounded angry, upset, emotionally spent, and beyond frustrated with his life. We spent two hours on the phone as he walked me through the pain of his church-soaked past.

Pete was raised in a Christian home and attended a Christian college, where he still felt emotionally disconnected from the opposite sex. He knew that homosexuality was sin, but he couldn't seem to prevent himself from wishing it wasn't. One evening after chapel, he attended a "Guys' Accountability" session, where his guilt and frustration finally became too much for him to bear. He opened up about his struggles to the Christian student leaders, who subsequently laughed at, ridiculed, and maligned him.

Humiliated, ashamed, angry at God, and knowing that his world was about to be exposed, Pete abruptly left the school and moved to California.

Of course, such a drastic life change requires financing, and Pete was soon in need of money to survive. Like many young men and women in Southern California, he chose to become a model and before long was posing nude. From there, it was only a matter of time and money before he found himself surviving on his own exploitation, moving from mere modeling to movie after movie of homosexual porn. More on Pete later.

I have another friend who has a similar story. Donny was a highly intelligent kid with an incredible memory, which his pastor parents packed with Scripture. He was a good kid with good parents involved in a good church—until their family faced an internal crisis that rocked their lives and soon became known in the church. Donny's father was determined to be faithful both to his natural family and to his church family, so he continued to lead the church, and everything was fine, until their supervising denomination decided they couldn't continue in this way.

For reasons Donny prefers not to discuss, the denomination removed Donny's father from his pastoral role, and soon afterward, Donny's family began to fall apart. Confused, bitter, and angry, Donny, now a young man, began to plot the most productive way to get back at the Christians who destroyed his family. He knew men in the church who struggled, who were almost addicted to porn. He began to make porn movies and marketed them to the men in the church to get them hooked.

Of course, porn's destructive influence extends beyond people in the church who view porn. It can also be devastating to those who stand outside the church, performing or producing porn. So many of the tragic stories we hear are from people who used to follow God but who succumbed to the money and other lures of the porn industry.

The church must wake up both to those within the church who are struggling and to the men and women stranded outside the walls of the church—people who feel that God, let alone his people, could never love them after what they've done.

PART 2

WHAT CAN BE DONE ABOUT IT?

THREE

Honorable Men

Equipping Guys for Sexual Integrity

It was only a few blocks, but the other end of the French Quarter might as well have been miles away. It was spring break in New Orleans, the streets were packed with college-age partiers, and the debauchery had reached an all-time high. My friend Donald, a minister, and I were stuck among them and needed to get out. Quick.

We had just attended a New Orleans Saints game in the Superdome and had no idea we were going to be stepping into a raucous street party. A few minutes of the madness swirling around us, and both of us knew it was time to leave. Maybe it was because of the city's history of voodoo; maybe it was because of the half-naked women swirling in silk on the balconies above. Whatever it was, we bolted, or at least we tried.

The packed streets made navigation difficult. People were everywhere. Trying to be forceful enough to negotiate the

----

crowd and courteous enough to avoid starting a riot, Donald and I elbowed our way past revelers partying at fever pitch. It was the last night of finals for many of the university students, and, pass or fail, they wanted to go out celebrating.

The smell of beer infused the air, while the street stench from the previous night's partying added a stale, pungent aroma to the atmosphere. High above street level, lined along the apartment balconies, women revelers danced, flashing the crowd. Even if a woman was two blocks away, I could hear the crowd's salacious response when she flashed them. Spontaneous applause and cheers erupted in every direction every few seconds.

Vendors were making a killing selling everything from bottles of water to party hats. People snatched up the silliest trinkets as souvenirs, and those famous necklaces made of gaudy beads were constantly selling out.

Our best option was to make our way clear of the Quarter and catch one of the cabs emptying partiers onto the already jam-packed streets. Here we were trying to *leave* downtown; everyone else was trying to get in.

Lust does that. Here in New Orleans, it had drawn a crowd to witness a level of hedonism I didn't know existed.

Standing and waiting for a cab, I was torn as thoughts of these women flooded my mind. Not in a sexual sense; I was thinking about who they were. I thought of my own little girl at home and wondered if any dads knew their little girls were here, dancing. Each of them was once someone's princess.

While one side of me wanted to pray for the lost little girls around me, the other side of me began to fill with lust. I was being drawn in, tempted to stop and stare. The war inside me lasted only a fraction of a second, but the tension lingered. If I'm totally honest, I had been visually captivated. I would like to believe it was more out of curiosity than perversion, but regardless, I was still drawn by it all.

This is nothing new; lust is deep-seated in the heart of man.

Think Adam.[1]
Think Noah.[2]
David.[3]
Paul.[4]

Though we waited only a few minutes for a cab, it felt like months. Each second was an hour, and I spent each of those hours engulfed in a war of conscience and conviction, between my commitment to guard my mind and a strong call to take mental snapshots.

As Donald and I finally sped away in our cab, I realized I had seen too much. I began to replay images of the women who bartered their modesty and purpose for cheap beads and momentary applause. A spark I should have doused was left unattended, and a fire began to stir, threatening to burn like a wildfire out of control.

The cab ducked down a side alley to navigate around a street that was closed, and I sat silent, my conscience seared. My flesh screamed, "Go back!" My spirit was confused. Though I had many unanswered questions, two gripped me the most. What in the world would cause a college-aged woman to strip, dance, and beckon the applause of drunken males for any price? And worse, why was I drawn to it?

Thought Prison

Nineteen hundred years ago Paul the apostle wrote these simple words: "Take captive every thought" (2 Cor. 10:5). These words are an encouragement to arrest every fleeting thought that may lead you away from Christ's perfect plan.

All thoughts in themselves aren't bad. Paul knew this, which is why he tells us to take them captive, to dwell on the good ones, the ones that will lead us closer to Christ, and remove the bad ones, the ones that will lead us closer to sin. We have *both* kinds of thoughts—it's what we *do* with them that counts.

The battle of the mind is the root issue, the systemic cause of all moral failures.

So why did Paul instruct us to put every thought in jail? Because he knew the battle of the mind is the root issue, the systemic cause of all moral failures. The mind begins the process of every action we take. The mind produces a thought; the thought develops into an action; the action, repeated over time, becomes a habit.

The process is subtle. So in that moment during my New Orleans cab ride, I had to ask myself a third question: *Am I willing to arrest the thoughts that are producing an insane magnetism toward unhealthy action?*

The problem is this: though we *can* choose to do the right thing, many times we *don't*. Again, consider Paul. He looked out over the people of Rome, a pagan city ruled by tyranny, a place filled with every sexual perversion, and acknowledged his own frailties. Allow me to paraphrase Romans 7:18–19: "The very things I should run away from and have no part of are the things I embrace. And the things I should make a regular part of my life I ignore."

Have you ever felt that way? I have. I did in that cab.

Can this process of going in the wrong direction be remedied? Is there hope? Is it possible to continue to choose the right road? Can we, as men, change? Is there a way to combat the feeling that failure is inevitable?

The answer, in all cases, is yes.

King David

You remember King David and his moral failure. This part of his story is told in 2 Samuel 11 and 12, and it begins with King David shirking his duty and hanging around the house instead of going out to war with his army. While he's up on the roof of the palace, he ogles Bathsheba, out bathing on her roof.

He's smitten, has her brought to the palace, commits adultery, and gets her pregnant. But she's married. His solution? King David has Bathsheba's husband placed in a vulnerable position so he is killed in battle. Then David can marry Bathsheba on the sly, and they can pretend the kid was conceived in the bonds of holy matrimony.

A baby boy is born, and God, displeased with David's actions, allows the unnamed child to become ill. Seven days later the child dies, and David is heartbroken. And it all happened because he looked. With a glimpse, he had a thought. The thought became an action. The action became a heartbreaking, twisted tale of sin and seduction.

King David shouldn't have been home in the first place—he should have been leading his army in battle. When he was on the roof, he shouldn't have gazed at Bathsheba. When he saw her, he shouldn't have had her brought to the palace. By that point, he'd already made up his mind to give in to his lust.

In David's story we see a progression, and with every step along that progression, he has a chance to take his thoughts captive, to take a stand against his sinful self, to turn around and go the other way. But the farther you let sin guide you, the more difficult it becomes to make the right choices.

> *The farther you let sin guide you, the more difficult it becomes to make the right choices.*

The most practical advice I've found in my years of working in this area is this: take the thought captive. And if you don't take the first thought captive, take the next one captive. It's never too late to put your thoughts in jail—ever. Sometimes it feels like porn use is so all-consuming, so prevalent in our society, there's no way you can *not* use it. It feels inevitable, so you might as well cave.

But you can always take a thought captive. Always. The Bible tells us in 1 Corinthians 10:13: "No temptation has seized you except what is common to man. And God is faithful; he will not let you be tempted beyond what you can bear. But when you are tempted, he will also provide a way out so that you can stand up under it."

I'll be blunt. Either you believe the Bible or you don't. Either you believe God really is going to give you a way out or you think he's lying to you. When I sat in that taxicab, riding back to my hotel with Donald, my mind on erotic autopilot, I had to make a decision. I decided to believe God and I chose to put a clamp on my thoughts. And you know what? God was faithful and really did provide a way out for me. Instead of a story of downfall, it's now a story of victory in my personal life.

Ways to Take the Thought Captive

Following are some helpful and practical ways every man should consider in his effort to take the thought captive.

IDENTIFY THE LEVEL OF ADDICTION

It is crucial to understand the severity of the porn consumption and the depth of the addiction. Even the slightest exposure can prompt a rapid downward spiral. Here is a simple scale we have found to be helpful:

0 The person has never been exposed to porn and would not know what it is.
1 The person has had brief exposure to some visual stimuli but is unaware of the effects of full nudity.
2 The person has had exposure to full sexual content and is curious about it; when viewed, an internal urge desires more.
3 The person has viewed porn and has a lingering desire for it. If given an opportunity, the person will engage with it.
4 The person thinks about porn, pursues it, hides it, wants it, and consumes it regularly.
5 The person can't go a day without it.

You may not always be at the same place on the scale. Your interest can fluctuate or accelerate depending on many external and internal factors. Some people take the long road to porn addiction; others have progressed from 0 to a full-fledged 5 in less than seventy-two hours. Once a person is at a 4 or higher, successful, lasting freedom from the addiction will require outside help, from a counselor, pastor, or accountability partner; sometimes lasting freedom comes only after a humiliating exposure of the sin.

PROTECT YOUR COMPUTER WITH ACCOUNTABILITY SOFTWARE

The anonymity and instantaneous nature of the internet makes it the perfect vehicle for both porn producers and users, which means that porn is readily available online. Anyone with access to the internet needs a protective shield, and what better one than the X3watch software? It's free, it works with both PCs, Macs, and iPhones/iPods and iPads, and it gives you the all-important tool of accountability.

With a simple online download, X3watch keeps a log of the questionable websites you visit, and if one of those sites has the possibility of questionable content, it records your visit. After two weeks, the software generates a list of those recorded sites of concern and emails it to your accountability partners—the one or two people you have predetermined as safe and strong people who will ask you, "Why was this site visited?" Often just knowing others will see their surfing patterns is enough to keep people from yielding to temptation.

In conjunction with X3, computers can also be loaded with up-to-date filtering software, a great tool to prevent certain pornographic sites from being visited. Filters and X3watch accountability work great together.

We have included a free thirty-day trial for Safe Eyes on the CD that is included in the book. You can get more information on X3watch and Safe Eyes on www.x3watch.com.

Seek Personal Accountability

In addition to the accountability provided through X3watch, you should give someone permission to ask you at any time the hard questions about your use of pornography. This must be a person you trust , and who, preferably, is also inviting you into *his* or *her* world. It should be someone who will not let you off the hook if you admit to using porn. While you need to be open and honest with your spouse, your spouse should not be the only person holding your accountable.

Personal accountability has helped many people stay on the path of integrity. Finding the right person is key. It should be a friend/spouse/mentor with whom you can talk about your struggles but someone who will hold you to your commitments. Often as accountability partners learn to trust each other, the comfort level grows and conversations can encompass many aspects of life, not just the problem with porn. This may lead to productive discussions of other problem areas of life.

Avoid Lingering in Lust

When confronted with a seemingly unavoidable situation where you find lust is pounding, try to get out of the environment quickly. When we view women as objects, we give ourselves permission to lust after them. Many are convinced that this is normal, but we know that this is not how

God wants us to see women. To acknowledge women are beautiful creations of God is understandable—staring at, lingering around, lusting for, and drooling over a woman is demeaning, both to her and to you. Taking steps to avoid lingering in lust will help you avoid all-out failure.

Guard your eyes and avoid environments where you will be susceptible to sin.

Jesus said that if you are lust filled, you are committing adultery in your heart (see Matt. 5:28). If you allow those thoughts to run rampant in your mind, it is only a matter of time before they lead to actions. Instead, guard your eyes and avoid environments where you will be susceptible to sin.

Develop Wholesome Relationships with Women

When we acknowledge that women are God's priceless and pure creations, we have a better chance at having wholesome relationships with them. For years, I have challenged men to look at women with pure intent, remembering that a woman may be someone's wife and is definitely someone's daughter. If a man has a daughter, he will be more inclined to understand this. Hopefully, for any man, character and compassion will prevail, his heart will be paternal, and a protective instinct will guard his thoughts and intentions toward women.

In wholesome relationships with women, men have an *agape* (or unconditional) love. Rather than looking at each woman with the intent of sexual conquest, stop that objectification short by thinking of the woman in terms of her family or friendship relationships.

Reason for Hope

But what if you've fallen? Is there any way to get back up? We've created some resources to help, like the X3pure program, a thirty-day online recovery program (see www.x3pure.com for more information). We also have two books, one written specifically for men called *Pure Eyes: A Man's Guide to Sexual Integrity* and one for women called *Pure Heart: A Woman's Guide to Sexual Integrity.*

But recovery begins with acceptance. After his failure with Bathsheba, King David crawled into a private place with God. He wrote out his apology and redirected his life plan. It's called Psalm 51. In the midst of his despair, David became willing to accept the consequences of his clandestine behavior, crying out for change that he knew would cost him everything.

God listened to him and had mercy on David and Bathsheba. And because of David's repentant heart, God gave them a second son, named Solomon. From Solomon's family line, Jesus eventually came.

It's never too late for God to redeem the life of a sinner. There will always be consequences for sin—some of them very rough. But God's redemption is always worth it.

So where are you in relationship to porn and sexual temptation?

Maybe you are like me. You too would have felt tension in New Orleans.

Maybe you identify with one of the confessors in the previous chapter.

Maybe you are like David.

Maybe you fantasize about women, and intimacy with your spouse has grown dormant.

Maybe you are living as an imposter.

Maybe your kids see you one way and you are living another way.

Maybe it is time to change.

There is hope.

There will *always* be hope.

Feminine Wholeness

Equipping Women
for Sexual Integrity

It may have been the case in the past, but these days it is simply naive to think porn usage is limited to men. In years past many thought the way the male visually processed information led to addiction, but increasingly women are sinking into the same addiction patterns as men.

Women have long seen the effects of porn on society, sometimes fearing it, sometimes wondering whether their man used it, sometimes curious about it. Soccer moms and strippers, power brokers and pastors' wives, all kinds of women are falling prey to their sexual curiosity.

The road to becoming hooked can begin in many different ways. Perhaps a woman's partner admitted to using porn, or maybe she caught him. She was infuriated that someone she loved had turned to an outside stimulus. But in time her own curiosity and wonder enticed her to see and explore what the big deal was. Why was it attractive to him? How attractive could it be?

In chapter 2, I listed some stats about porn use by Christian women, but they bear repeating here. These stats shocked me when I first heard them. The poll was conducted in the summer of 2006. Of the Christian women polled, 20 percent admitted they were addicted to pornography, 60 percent admitted to having significant struggles with lust, and four out of ten admitted to being involved in sexual sin in the past year.[1] Make no mistake; porn is a problem among women, even Christian women.

Following are the stories of two women who have different struggles related to the same problem: porn.

Meet Terri and Crissy.

Terri's Discovery

Terri was a faithful woman. She grew up in the church and attended a Christian school, so she had always been guarded with her sexuality. Aside from a few nights as a teenager when she had gone a bit too far with her boyfriend, Terri had remained sexually pure and was completely committed to her two-year-old marriage. She felt secure.

"I remember the first day he suggested it," she told me. "I thought he was joking, but then he turned to the late-night cable channel to show me a skin flick."

Terri slowed down, reflecting, and chose her words carefully as she described the way their sex life had become routine and predictable, only two years into their marriage.

"I remember thinking then that every couple probably uses some porn to spice things up a bit. Looking back at my shattered dreams, I hope I am wrong."

While not every couple views porn together to "enhance their sex life," many married couples admit to using it, though recent research has revealed that 42 percent of adults feel insecure about their partner's pornography use, and almost the same number feel less attractive for the same reason.[2]

Confused but wanting to please her husband, Terri let him introduce porn into their marriage. "When we started to have sex," she said, "I would catch him looking over my shoulder to glance at the television screen. He was focused more on the screen than he was on me."

Her voice began to crack with emotion. "The intimacy we had died. I felt violated but I didn't say anything. I just kept allowing it, fearing that if I stopped, he would watch it without me there."

Terri's insights are common. Many women believe the only way to keep their husband in their bed is to allow him to set the ground rules. But if he is not committed to his own convictions, his marriage covenant, and his purity, those ground rules can be most anything and will be loosely applied.

As time passed, the suggestions and selections of porn they watched became gradually more raw, and in less than a month from her first exposure, her husband was no longer flipping to late-night HBO. He was offering DVDs he said he'd picked up from the guys at work.

Perplexed and embarrassed at the thought that she was not able to satisfy her husband, Terri sat one day and cried as the chaos of her marriage and the sabotage of her marital intimacy crushed her. What did the videos offer her husband that she had not been able to supply?

> *If a man is not committed to his own convictions, his marriage covenant, and his purity, his ground rules can be most anything and will be loosely applied.*

While cleaning the house one day, this very question lured her to the leather attaché case she found in the back of her husband's side of the closet. Barely visible, the brown sheen of the briefcase called to Terri. As she reached for it, anxiety and angst gripped her. Was her husband hiding something? She had to know. She was only curious. She wasn't planning to fall headlong into porn's sensuous and seductive trap.

Crissy, the Rising Star

The air was thick with the heat and smog of the San Fernando Valley. On a side street off a main drag of Simi Valley was a row of unmarked doors, a business park housing any number of low-end small businesses. One of these doors opened up to one of the thousands of businesses profiting from the broken and the hurting.

Crissy was inside, making her latest movie.

From childhood Crissy had been in and out of relationships with people who took advantage of her. Whether by a drug-addicted boyfriend who acted as a pimp or by some bottom-feeder in the porn industry, Crissy was victimized . . . often.

Growing up in Jacksonville, Florida, she received affection and affirmation from her father, a pastor of a local church.

But while he delivered fiery sermons on the weekends, the rest of the week he craved the fire in his stomach that only alcohol could deliver. Meaning well, he warned Crissy to do as he said not as he did, but in time the shame of his hypocrisy led him to withdraw from his family.

This subtle paternal silence drove the already naturally shy Crissy to question the value of her place in the world. When her father was drunk, he railed against Crissy and those around her, and whoever was in earshot heard of his daughter's virginity and how he would kill any man who took it.

Crissy believed it; so did those who took the indirect threats personally. But the constant mention of the subject created in her mind the awareness of her sexuality, and she could feel men looking at her with lust. To this day Crissy admits she is insecure about her looks and hates to be seen without her makeup.

When Crissy was in ninth grade, she and her mom moved out to escape the unpredictable behavior of her dad, and by the end of high school, the once shy Crissy, needing the love of a father, began looking for that love in the arms of men around her.

At the age of eighteen, Crissy was leading a promiscuous life. "I would have wild nights from time to time where I would drink a lot to get through the pain in my life. I would hurt myself to see if anyone would care . . . and no one did." She became pregnant and decided to have an abortion. Because of her lifestyle, her mother kicked her out of the house, so she was on her own, trying to make ends meet in Los Angeles. Hoping to break into modeling, Crissy posted photos of herself in a bikini on the web. Within hours her email in-box was flooded with messages loaded with affirmation and affection from willing photographers. The responses soothed Crissy's insecurities.

She was in and out of relationships. She and a man got engaged but broke it off. She was so wrecked that she began having panic attacks and got on medication to control them, which dulled *all* her emotions.

One day, bored at work, she cruised the internet and found a modeling website, where she posted some pictures of herself. Soon she got a job doing a topless shoot. On day two she went completely naked.

Crissy's popularity in the modeling world began to rise. Her new boyfriend managed her nude modeling career, while simultaneously using compliments, promises of payoff, and a battery of drugs to chip away at what was left of her crumbling conscience. He led her to do things she had never dreamed she would do. "The more you open your mind," he would say, "the more money you could make."

She took the step into porn. Straight guy sex escalated into threesomes with other women, then into simulated bondage and more.

Crissy hated what she was doing, hated herself for doing it. But she felt trapped, with a controlling boyfriend who gave her nowhere else to go. "He controlled my modeling career, my emails, my phone calls, my friendships, my bank account, my life!" She joined her boyfriend in doing cocaine, crystal meth, marijuana, and ecstasy. And all the while her boyfriend used porn and chased other women. That hurt.

He used violence to control her. "One day he tried to smother me with my pillow. After hours of arguing I ran out of the house and down the street to a neighbor's house. They called the police and he went to jail. I tried to make plans to leave, but his friends posted bail and he came home before I could get away."

While her personal world was falling apart, Crissy's professional world was skyrocketing. Calls continued to come in from high-level XXX magazines and porn producers, and Crissy parlayed her thriving porn career into a lucrative web presence that made her fourteen thousand dollars a month.

All the cash deadened her conscience, and in the midst of all her success, she experienced what became a personal and professional low for her when "Mike," a porn producer, hired her for a bondage shoot in Los Angeles.

"The room was cold and the music was loud," she remembers, "with the darkest lyrics I have ever heard. [Mike] meticulously bound my arms together and tied them from the ceiling. He tied my right leg from another rope that extended from the ceiling. I stood there on my left foot in the highest arched high heels I have ever worn, slightly leaning forward and held up by the ropes from the ceiling. I was so tightly bound that I felt a slight tingle in every limb. He told me the vision he had in his mind. He then grabbed a Ball-Gag, popped it into my mouth, and buckled it behind my head. He touched my chin with his finger and told me I looked good with a Ball-Gag in my mouth. He walked away to grab his camera and adjust the lights, then said the words I will never forget: 'Okay, struggle.' I felt the darkness envelop me."

Crissy's money could not buy her comfort, peace, or the true, authentic love she longed for. The more she continued in the industry, the more desperate she felt, and the more she thought of finding her own way out through suicide. Crissy dodged the drug addiction that many in the industry battle, though she did use drugs to mask the pain she felt as she performed for the cameras. The more explicit the sex scene, the more drugs she used—a common practice in the industry to deaden the senses.

Many in the porn industry struggle with the same feelings, trying to convince others that everything is okay while they're dying on the inside. There's almost a survival camaraderie that develops among performers, even between Crissy and Mike, the bondage producer. "He later became my friend," she recounted. "I saw the softer side of him that not many saw. I found out later he too was suffering. But I didn't realize it until it was too late. He ended up in jail and hung himself with his bedsheet. I never got to say good-bye."

Terri's Plunge

Terri knelt in the closet and opened the bag her husband had hidden there. Inside she found stacks of DVDs, and with each title she read, another piece of her confidence and marital security crumbled. When she had read them all, her once pure and wholly devoted love to her husband had been completely leveled.

Curiosity courted her as she shuffled through the thirty or so DVDs, some with stereotypical porn themes—knockoffs of popular Hollywood movies but with a pornographic twist. Other titles were more sinister. Fetish, girl-on-girl, and even a few that dove deeper into the dark side of the industry.

Flushed, frustrated, but now interested, she carried the case to the nearest TV and loaded in one DVD after another. She could only stomach a minute or two of each disc before ripping it out of the player and throwing it back into the satchel. Within an hour or so, she had looked at most of them.

Sitting there in shock, contemplating what was going on, Terry felt strangely divided. One part of her was disgusted that her husband found pleasure in such films, while another part began to be aroused.

"I thought, *I could perform like them*. It didn't seem natural, but if my husband wanted me to, I could scream, holler. I would even bark like a dog. Or at least I would try. But while I was thinking this, my confidence and self-esteem were destroyed."

Terri began to simmer with rage. "I felt anger at the women on the screen. I was mad at my husband, but I wanted to kill the women."

There was a single DVD left in the bag, and a sudden thought leaped into her mind as she loaded it into the player: if it worked for him, maybe it would work for her. Illogical and desperate, Terri opened her mind to the thought that maybe it was normal for her to feel slightly aroused. The blondes on the screen were certainly making bisexuality and overt acts of lesbianism look normal.

Whether it was for revenge or rebellion as a payback tool, Terri let herself be lured. In the back of her mind, she wondered if her husband's fascination and addiction had started off in a similar way. She was thirty. He had been thirteen.

When she finished watching, Terri repacked the DVDs and slid the bag back into its hiding place in the dark closet. The same anxiety that had gripped her when she found the stash also held her as she walked away from it.

When her husband got home from work, Terri found she had a bigger dilemma than her husband's addiction. "If I tell him what I had found, how can I tell him what I had done?" In that moment she realized her marriage would never be the same.

Crissy Finds Promise

Crissy did not think her career in porn would last more than six years. Like so many others who are trapped in the industry, she thought she would just do a few jobs to make a little quick cash and then transition into mainstream acting and modeling. But despite the effect porn was having on her soul, the money and affirmation were impossible for her to ignore.

Oddly enough, her first step out the door of the porn world came when she saw the way lust and the use of porn negatively affected her boyfriend. "My eyes were opened to see how lust in general affected my relationships. This made me reflect on what it was I was doing. It made me think of how the porn could affect my fans and their wives."

Crissy needed to connect to hope, and it came in the form of Chris, a friend of a friend. While sitting in a bar, Crissy and a group of friends were talking about girls, her career, and the porn industry.

"The conversation around the table had been about showing off pictures of me," Crissy remembers. "My boyfriend had done that, and I said, 'When I get married, I want to marry a man who would love me enough not to show me off.'"

Chris responded quickly, "I wouldn't show my wife off." He had Crissy's attention. From that point on, Crissy was interested in whatever Chris wanted to talk about, and over their next series of conversations, Chris reintroduced Crissy to the God who had so faithfully chased her when she was growing up. Within two months Crissy had decided her porn career was done. She walked away from the lucrative business of porn and into a consistent and growing relationship with Christ.

But porn wasn't done with her. Crissy's many websites were owned by others, including a man who absolutely hated God. He told Crissy that if she had left to be a mom or to get another job, he would have pulled the sites. But because he hated her choice to pursue God, he was going to keep them up.

Crissy was under contract, but Christ meant more to her than money. To show she was serious, she refused to take the profits from the porn she had helped create.

The message boards that chatted about the porn industry poked at her conversion and transformation. And although the money was gone, the images and videos of Crissy's six-year career remained in circulation, and the internet masses began to seethe about her decision. God-haters posted Photoshopped images of Jesus printed on her breast. It hurt. But this time *the pain had purpose*, and since her decision, Crissy has not received one penny from the porn industry.

Today Crissy seeks solace away from the industry. It took an extreme level of commitment for her to walk away as she did. Producers' affections, addictions, money, the need to belong, and admiration from fans are powerful magnets that hold so many captive. The industry lets every actor and actress go at some point, but it always wants to dictate the terms.

As her pain slowly gave way to promise, Crissy's relationship with God began to deepen. "I struggle daily with my past mistakes, not because I feel condemned, because I know there is no condemnation in Christ. I remember learning this but to believe it is a whole other thing. I worry that my past will lead others down the wrong path. It causes me so much grief to think that other young women might see my past and be persuaded to get involved in porn. It's painful to think that my old images are fuel to someone addicted to porn."

While faithfully attending a church in Southern California, Crissy is seeking the continued restoration that only God can bring. Each day she seeks to do the right thing in every aspect of life, but it's a journey that often requires two steps forward and one step back. Sometimes it is one step forward and two steps back. But she is committed.

Terri's World Collapses

Terri walked down the stairs to welcome her husband home, her mind flashing mental slides of all the times her church had blasted homosexuality and she had applauded. She recalled with vivid details the instances when she'd chatted with her "sisters in the Lord" at a Bible study, passing judgment against the Crissys of the world who were nothing more than "brazen hussies" who destroyed marriages.

Now she had embraced the very thing she despised. Porn had affected her husband. Porn had affected her. It had affected them as a couple, and she wasn't ready to give it up.

With agonizing anxiety, Terri decided to keep her mouth shut, ignoring the inevitable need for a conversation and telling herself it was to save the marriage. She greeted her husband with a happy face, convinced that she had to work through on her own the pain of the questions in her mind.

But there was a deeper reason for her silence. Curiosity tapped a deep root inside of her, and the next day she found herself reaching for the case in the back of the closet—and the day after that, and the day after that. Every day, at some point, she locked the doors, got out the satchel, and watched the DVDs. Subtle interest turned to methodical pursuit, and Terri felt helpless to stop it.

Six months after her discovery of the satchel, she made a mistake—she forgot to close the bag correctly. When her husband saw it and asked her about it, she told him the whole story, though she thought it was a horrible indictment on her as a wife. Instead, her husband blew it off and suggested they continue to use porn to "spice things up."

It didn't work, though, as both Terri and her husband felt insecure about their ability to satisfy each other. As porn played out on their flat-screen TV in the bedroom, she wondered if he was aroused by the girls on the screen; he wondered if she was fantasizing about the guy, never dreaming her thoughts were turning to the other women. The room that was supposed to represent intimacy between them was now filled with other people.

One day Terri had had enough and confessed to him. Bad became worse, and they hit rock bottom. With nowhere else to go, they took a long hard look at their relationship and sought some outside help. Now, through Christian intervention, counseling, and safety parameters on their marriage, Terri and her husband are slowly reassembling the pieces of their shattered lives.

Gateways to Porn

Two women, one theme: lives derailed by the business of seduction.

So how do we make sense of all this? Both Crissy and Terri knew what they were doing was wrong. Somewhere along the way they lost sight of a bigger picture of purity, commitment, and covenant.

How can this happen? Most of the time women involved with porn do not mean to get trapped. But somehow a few steps toward porn can become a trip down a slippery slope.

There are many gateways leading to this slippery slope, and regardless of the one that is entered, a person will quickly lose her footing that is nearly impossible to regain. Following are a few of the gateways that pertain to porn and are particularly effective in drawing women.

Television

Television programs, such as soap operas, *Sex and the City*, *Desperate Housewives*, and *The Real Housewives of Orange County*, provide a gateway to fantasy and escapism. The bed-hopping images they offer tell women it's natural to be involved in a supersex-charged world.

Books

Harlequin Romance novels of the 1970s are G-rated compared to the romance fiction available today. And if you think no one is reading it, guess again. In the United States 1.37 billion dollars' worth of romance fiction was sold in the year 2008 and had by far the largest share of genre fiction on the market.[3] Explicit sexual writing found in trashy romance novels and even in many bestsellers can lead women to lose their sexual inhibitions and be willing to explore new possibilities for their sex life.

Prescription and Illicit Drug Abuse

Addiction specialists explain that introducing drugs to a person in an illicit fashion affects the thinking process. In opiate-based drug use, euphoria and altered mood states often lower inhibitions, which can and often does lead to sexual experimentation. Enter porn.

Philippians 4:8 says that to maintain a healthy thought life, people, both men and women, are to meditate on pure things. Gateways silence such instructions, pushing us to meditate on the lies of our media culture.

> *Explicit sexual writing found in trashy romance novels and even in many bestsellers can lead women to lose their sexual inhibitions and be willing to explore new possibilities for their sex life.*

Guidelines for Wholeness

Often those of us who speak up about the porn battle address the effects porn has on a man, and most porn recovery resources are directed at men. Few recovery movements help women understand the problem and cope with the fallout that comes from their porn-interrupted relationship.

When a husband is unfaithful—and porn use is as bad as adultery (Matt. 5:27–28)—the wife cannot avoid the shrapnel that flies from the indiscretion. She feels the guilt and asks, *What could I have done to prevent this?* She's overwhelmed with insecurities, and in the recesses of her mind she wonders where she was lacking. Why did he turn to porn instead of her?

This question cannot be answered because porn use has nothing to do with finding sexual fulfillment and everything to do with indulging lust. It's the same reason we tend to reach for the bag of chips instead of the bag of baby carrots when we're hungry, or that we let ourselves act in anger in the midst of an argument and say something we neither mean nor believe.

Porn has become common in our culture and often feels inescapable. The following are some guidelines for help and wholeness.

Control Curiosity

You don't need to be an expert or even knowledgeable about cancer to know it kills. And you don't have to be familiar with porn to know it has no redeeming value. Like Terri, many women tell us their initial exposure to porn came through curiosity. Essentially, women want to know why it lures so many men and through their investigation of it fall victim to its snare.

Keep a Healthy Perspective

The best way to avoid being lured by porn is by keeping a healthy perspective and focus on purity and God's perfect plan for your life. Women who believe that a person in a film, the handsome soccer dad down the road, or another woman can be more fulfilling than a God-centered relationship with their spouse are believing a falsehood.

Porn use has nothing to do with finding sexual fulfillment and everything to do with indulging lust.

Recognize Porn's Emptiness

Porn glitters and looks appealing but it is not of value and it has no worth. As we learned from Crissy, the majority of the people performing in porn are trapped in a cycle of shame and self-hatred. They'll talk about how great they feel or how much fun they're having or how they love to "party," but in the end they're just acting. They are performers and they're very good at hiding the hurt and pain inside them.

Don't Underestimate the Power of Porn

Porn will always take you farther than you want to go. What seems to be a quick glance will eventually turn into a journey of long looks—and many years. It may start with only a moment of indulgence, but in time, without fail, people find they are in a pit too big to get out of on their own.

The best way to avoid getting lost in porn is never to take a turn into it in the first place. Make a commitment with yourself, your spouse (if you're married), and your accountability partner not to give porn even an inch. And if you do, remember that when you confess your sin, God is "faithful and just and will forgive us our sins and purify us from all unrighteousness" (1 John 1:9). Get yourself back on the right road immediately and let God do his purification work.

Face the Truth

Many people gain surface-level comfort by putting their fingers in their ears, placing their heads in the sand, and hoping their difficulty will go away. This is true for many hooked by porn. They are not willing to admit that they have a problem.

The very fact that you're reading this book means you're probably willing to acknowledge that something is wrong, but it may be that you are not at the place where you are willing to do anything about it. Remember that it's a lie to say to yourself, *I would be better off accepting this than facing the hardship of fighting it.* Those wanting true freedom have discovered this truth: bad news that is real is better than good news that is fake.

Acknowledge Your Sin

The reality comes down to an acknowledgment of sowing and reaping. Whatever seeds you put in the ground, that's the type of fruit you're going to get. You may not be aware of all the consequences of the decisions you're making for yourself, but eventually you will have to deal with them one way or another. Acknowledge that indulgence in pornography is sin and ask God to help you eliminate it from your life.

Take Responsibility for Your Behavior

Each person makes choices about what she will do. Blaming others for our choices is easy but unrealistic. Terri pointed fingers at women like Crissy and other "brazen hussies" for a long time, but in the end she had to recognize her own responsibility for her actions.

Your decisions are *your* decisions, and you'll be held accountable for them. What others do cannot dictate your actions. Remember what Jesus said: "Do not judge, or you too will be judged.

> *Bad news that is real is better than good news that is fake.*

For in the same way you judge others, you will be judged, and with the measure you use, it will be measured to you. Why do you look at the speck of sawdust in your brother's eye and pay no attention to the plank in your own eye?" (Matt. 7:1–3). If each of us makes a commitment to become the best version of ourselves, we can do what is right and see freedom.

Have an Accountability Partner

If you don't have anyone asking you the hard questions and keeping you accountable, you're opening yourself up to deception through omission. People are able to deceive themselves and others when no one ever asks them, "Hey, is everything all right?"

Instead, get someone in your life who can remind you of your commitment to purity. If you noticed, neither Terri nor Crissy had someone like that in their life, someone who was invited to break down the wall of isolation and ask them the hard questions. Remember Proverbs 27:17: "As iron sharpens iron, so one man [or woman] sharpens another."

Do Drastic Cleansing

The battle is constant, and if you keep your porn on a shelf and tell yourself you won't use it, there will come a moment of weakness when you will take it down. Most who are dealing or dabbling in porn believe it can do no damage to the soul, but the reality is the opposite. Porn is not idle. It destroys every time it enters a mind and heart.

Get rid of it—every bit of it. Destroy the DVDs and the magazines. Put safeguards on your computer. Don't go near an adult bookstore. You need to take both feet out of the porn world and put them in God's world. Why would you hang onto it, anyway? What sense of security does it give you?

Know That You Were Wonderfully Made

Most women have had their self-confidence shaken by bouts with an unhealthy self-image, often wishing to be taller, shorter, thinner, rounder, have curlier hair, have straighter hair, have bigger or smaller body parts—the list goes on and on. Few are completely satisfied with themselves as they are.

How can you counter these self-image problems? You must accept and understand that God created you after the love and desires of his heart. This is easy to say but not so easy to do. It requires trust in God and his Word. Scripture says that we are "fearfully and wonderfully made" (Ps. 139:14). The more you focus on the fact that you are God's wonderful creation, the more you can become comfortable in your skin, and the less likely you are to think you must compete with the airbrushed and Photoshopped "perfection" presented in the pages of porn.

Nurture a Good Body Image

It seems apparent that people who have a commitment to healthy living tend to have a healthier self-perception and higher personal confidence. Studies have shown that women who work out, eat a healthy diet, and maintain consistent schedules are less likely to act compulsively or dwell on negative thoughts about themselves or others in their life. When the mind, body, and soul are synced up with energy and exercise, the harmful behavior that demands sexual promiscuity for acceptance becomes replaced with confidence and purpose, making women less likely to engage in porn usage, sexual exploration, and promiscuity.

Seek Sexual Wholeness

With the onslaught of sexually charged television, film, print media, and popular music, women are often treated as sexual objects. Whether desperate or sleazy, the objectified woman can be duped into believing that her value lies between her legs. Women in this trap can find an unhealthy significance in the power to persuade through sex. Porn acts, like an illicit tutor, prompt and coach women into an imaginary world that presents a false image of what healthy sex looks like.

Both Terri and Crissy were victims of porn's lies. When they turned away from the lies, they both discovered that God's plan for purity actually increased their ability to be intimate. Wholeness in their daily living reintroduced an accurate picture of what true love looks like.

The biblical instruction is clear: both men *and* women are challenged to meditate on the things that are true, noble, right, pure, lovely, admirable, excellent, and praiseworthy (see Phil. 4:8). Identify things, people, attitudes, and anything else in your life that are derailing this pursuit and eliminate them immediately.

If you're struggling, please investigate X3pure (www.x3 pure.com) and XXXchurch.com's book *Pure Heart*, written specifically for women.

Our world is filled with people whose stories echo those of Terri and Crissy. Regardless of which side of the industry, consumer or camera guy, actress or addict, if a person wants to be free, he or she must be committed to becoming all that God created him or her to be.

You can be that today.

FIVE

Good Sex

Protecting and Nurturing
Your Marriage

Marriages are difficult to maintain even *without* the looming threat of pornography, and just having faith is not enough to keep your marriage safe. Research from the Barna Group shows that there is no statistical difference between Christians and non-Christians who divorce.[1] Add to this already difficult challenge the burden of a pornography addiction, and the numbers are against you.

I hear stories almost daily about porn destroying a family. From the parent who found it in her kid's room to the dad who was caught by his wife, porn is detonating families, and XXXchurch has become a landing zone for the fallout.

The effects of porn on a marriage are devastating. It breaks trust, destroys intimacy, eats away at emotions, distracts couples from bonding at the deepest levels, and creates deviant patterns of unhealthy sexual desires.

Maybe your marriage is in a shambles because of porn use. You aren't alone. Marriage therapists report an increased number of clients presenting porn-related problems. For example, 50 percent of divorce cases in 2002 involved porn, according to *The Porn Trap* by authors Wendy and Larry Maltz.[2]

The use of porn breaks trust, destroys intimacy, eats away at emotions, distracts couples from bonding at the deepest levels, and creates deviant patterns of unhealthy sexual desires.

Recently this confession came to our website: "I am a 31-year-old wife and mother. I was sexually molested by an older boy and a woman when I was very young. It lasted about 8 years of my childhood. On top of that, I found porn that my dad had hidden in his room at the age of 12 and was instantly hooked. I will go several months, even years at times, without viewing porn or any form of erotic material. Then, all at once I begin to have very real, vivid dreams about sexual acts being done. I then find myself giving in and going to search out something to look at. Once that is done, I will go another several months without looking at anything. But I want to be free. I want my mind to be free. I want to be with my husband when we are together, not thinking of other things so I can become aroused. I want to be pure in heart and mind. I want to be a godly wife and mother, I want to be free. I don't know where to start really, so I'm starting here. I pray that through this site, God completely and totally sets me free."

Every day we see stories like this pouring in, stories of how porn has been instrumental in someone's devastation, of men messing up on their wives and wives messing up on their husbands. What can be done? It's crucial to take an honest look at yourself and your marriage to achieve greater intimacy; however, before you can build intimacy, you have to consider what porn does at the root level of a relationship.

Porn Breaks Trust

A healthy marriage is based on trust and intimacy. We see this in the Scripture that states, "a man should leave his mother and a woman leave her home and the two shall become one" (see Mark 10:7–8). These verses are all about leaving what *was* safe (your parents' house) and building something together that *is* safe (your house).

A man is raised from a young age to depend on his father's leadership and to trust in his mother's maternal nurturing, and when he marries, he must transfer his trust to his bride and their relationship, leaving behind his dependence on Dad and Mom. This is the first stepping-stone for a scriptural marriage.

What about a woman? God intended her to be raised in a home that was her safe place, where nothing could or should be able to hurt her. We know this isn't always the case, but that's the hope we have for all our children. Then Scripture instructs a woman to leave her home and shift her trust for safety to her husband.

Porn is a violation of trust, plain and simple. Remember the story of Terri? Her husband introduced porn into their marriage with devastating effects, and now they're still working on rebuilding the broken trust. If you're reading this with porn stashed in your home, car, office, or computer, it is only a matter of time before someone who trusts you finds it. And then what will become of that person's trust? Is it worth it?

The other scenario of broken trust happens when a spouse suggests bringing porn into the marriage, wanting to "spice things up." I have heard both husbands and wives confess they used this approach out of a selfish desire to indulge in porn. When one spouse trusts another and follows his or her suggestion, it is devastating to discover that the spouse who wanted to use porn did not have the best interests of the marriage or the other spouse at heart. Rather he or she was seeking a way to indulge lust.

Broken trust alters the very core of a relationship, and the only way to restore it is by making good decisions over time. However, I cannot say with certainty that trust can ever be *completely* restored in a marriage infested with porn, and without this vital marriage component, intimacy is almost impossible.

Porn Destroys Intimacy

Lee Wilson, director of media and literature for the Family Dynamic Institution, discussed the power of choice to enhance or decrease intimacy.

> If you choose to use pornography as a means to sexually arouse yourself, you are forfeiting the ability to become aroused by your spouse. Over time, it will become more and more dif-

ficult to be sexually aroused by your life-mate because he or she will age while the porn star forever remains youthful in pictures and videos.[3]

Rick Schatz, president of the National Coalition for the Protection of Children and Families, said porn demeans women, marriage, commitment, fidelity, and children.

It produces a distorted view of sexual relationships within the covenantal marriage relationship that God intended for one man and one woman. The use of porn totally divorces intimacy and commitment from the sexual relationship so that sex becomes nothing more than an act of self-fulfillment rather than a mutually satisfying and beautiful part of a committed relationship between one man and one woman.[4]

Porn lies, telling you that your spouse will never measure up to what porn has to offer. Once you believe that—and you *will* believe that—your intimacy is over. Fantasy eventually takes people farther away from their spouse than they wanted to go and offers no turnaround.

Porn Eats at Your Conscience

Porn doesn't just stop at breaking trust and destroying intimacy—it also works on exhausting your mind. Guilt becomes the motivating force in your life, and you'll spend endless amounts of emotion and creativity inventing story lines so you can lie effectively. Then you lie about the lies you lied about, and the truth becomes blurred.

But eventually people who indulge in porn will probably come to the place where they have to deal with guilt and their conscience will push them to confess.

Most people will do just that. Their guilt becomes unbearable. If they don't confess, they try to bury the memories of their behavior by making empty promises in their minds like, *What happened in Vegas stays in Vegas.* The more truthful statement is: What happened in Vegas can destroy your trusting family at home.

If they don't confess, their emotional turmoil will lead them to withdraw subconsciously from their marriage. This pullback begins to affect the innocent partner, as he or she begins to wonder what went wrong. *What did I do to cause the distance?* The person's self-worth plummets, and the distance between spouses grows even wider.

Jesus said in Matthew 5:27–28, "You have heard that it was said, 'Do not commit adultery.' But I tell you that anyone who looks at a woman lustfully has already committed adultery with her in his heart." Jesus was placing emphasis on how powerful the emotions and the mind can be. Essentially, Jesus stated that having an uncontrolled mind will inevitably lead to thoughts that become actions. It's the same way with porn.

Consider the cost versus the reward. Is it worth it?

One Couple's Story

I have a friend who learned this truth firsthand. He's a happy-go-lucky kind of guy. He called me to meet with him, and when I saw him, he looked tired and worn, a far stretch from his usual self. Only days earlier I had seen him at church with his wife, walking hand in hand, clutching their Bibles.

"I haven't slept in two days," he said. "Things are bad. I need help." Then he corrected himself and continued. "*We* need help. My wife and I."

He began to unpack his emotion and pain, and within an hour I had heard the depths of their tragic story. He had become an inferno of rage and anger. Jealousy at times drove him to berate his wife. Sometimes the neighbors would call because the sounds of his tirades would drift through their walls. The fighting had finally gotten so bad she couldn't take it anymore and had moved out that morning.

How had it come to this? They seemed so happy at church, and though they lived in Las Vegas, neither of them felt that the insidious Vegas culture had grabbed them. They thought that living away from The Strip protected them. Yet here they were, their marriage hanging by a thread.

It began with his headfirst dive into porn and the sex industry. His wife had no clue. At times he would call her and tell her he had to work late, but in reality he was headed to a strip bar across town so he could steer clear of anyone who would recognize him.

The dimly lit booths in any one of hundreds of strip clubs in Vegas offered the perfect cover. He parked in back so his car couldn't be seen, slithering in with lust on his mind and twenty or thirty bucks from the family budget in his pocket. There he could get his own private show.

"I felt like a dirty old man," he confessed to me. "The girls dancing were young enough to be my daughter." His face flinched with regret.

When he had become aroused, he would motion for a lap dance, a private dance given to a paying individual at their table or chair. At times he would get so caught up in the fantasy that, as the unknown woman with the intoxicating perfume danced for him, getting *just* close enough to almost touch, then backing away, he imagined they were having sex.

We have helped many dancers escape from this industry, and they've told us how they would do everything they could just short of a sexual act to get the man hooked (and therefore get more money from him). In fact many clubs are a cover for sex acts; this *is* Vegas, after all, and few people ever get busted.

With tears of regret filling his bloodshot eyes, my friend described to me how this was only the tip of the iceberg. Well within the emotional and sexual grasp of the dancer, he would often ejaculate in his closed pants. Many times he had to sneak into his house and quickly change to avoid his wife's detection.

More than one night he said no to sex with his wife, his guilt from his tryst only hours before still plaguing him. Sometimes he agreed, but he would go flaccid before either of them would achieve orgasm. She began to wonder what was wrong with her, why she could no longer interest her husband sexually.

And this was only the beginning. Trying to "spice things up" and avoid another rejection from her husband, my friend's wife decided to make him an offer he could not refuse. Coming home from work, he entered the house and heard voices in the kitchen. His wife was talking to one of her longtime friends from high school. He offered a quick hello and was stunned when his wife blatantly described what she had in mind: the two women had decided a third party in the marriage bed would make things more interesting.

From here, the story derailed into a tale of two best friends hating each other, a wife living outside her home, a possible divorce, and out-of-control thoughts assaulting my friend's mind as he obsessed over whether his wife and her friend had ever been sexually involved before.

What will happen to them? Only time will tell.

This is one of hundreds of stories we hear, stories of how the trickle-down effects of porn strangle life from marriage.

Keys to Building a Healthy Marriage

Though porn destroys marriages, it takes more than just not using porn to keep your marriage growing, healthy, and strong. Here are some keys to assist you as you strive to keep your marriage thriving.

Set Healthy Parameters

God has given us parameters throughout Scripture to help us keep our lives pure and our love strong. Parameters are not meant to fence people in but to protect that which is priceless. Set healthy parameters for your relationship that deal with the day-to-day interactions of life so you will not fall victim to subtle traps that can destroy. Many of these parameters are good ideas for everyone, but they're especially crucial for married people.

Guard Your Eyes

With so much sensual material in this world, commit yourself to guarding your eyes from anything that causes your thoughts to wander to impurity. When you are with your spouse, focus on the desire you have for each other. Don't allow unhealthy glances or wandering eyes. Television shows and even some television ads can produce impure thoughts that lead to unhealthy behavior. Turn them off before you get hooked. Sticking to this guideline will take guts and willpower.

Guard Your Associations

The behavior of those you spend time with becomes your behavior, and bad company corrupts good character. If your friends are consumed with talking about sexual escapades or exploitive behavior, get new friends. Get away from those who suggest taking part in immorality. Take charge of the relational environments in which you place yourself.

Guard Your Ears

Inappropriate words masked as flirtatious compliments are stepping-stones toward irreversible effects. I have seen relationships destroyed because a wife was innocently seduced by a friend's listening ear and kind words. I have also known men and women who have mastered making comments that lead to more aggressive flirtatious behavior. Don't allow it. If someone makes a comment to you that is flirty or over the edge, make it immediately clear this is not acceptable behavior. If it happens twice, bring your spouse into the loop and talk about it.

Guard Your Time and Money

Friends of ours who have struggled with porn have taken steps to control their use of time and money. They have asked their spouses to control the money and made themselves accountable to a friend for the ways they spend their time. The formula is simple and it works as a healthy parameter. If there is strict accountability of money (no cash in hand) and time (where have you been and what have you been doing?), it is much more difficult to get in a place that leads to trouble.

Work at Romance

Did you know it's important to keep dating even though you're married? It's easy to let time pass and allow dating and romance in your marriage to disappear, but then you're setting yourself up for boredom and the inevitable desire to seek out something new. Instead, set up date nights with each other. They don't have to be expensive, just creative. Your calendar should have at least one date night a month. Remind each other and plan ahead so you have something to look forward to. Even a movie night at home with take-out food can keep the love spark glowing.

> *Keep dating even though you're married.*

According to a 2003 *Newsweek* study, between 15 and 20 percent of couples are living in a sexless marriage—couples who make love no more than ten times a year.[5] While sex is not the be-all and end-all in a marriage, it is obviously one of the best ways to maintain intimacy. Most men think sex has to be daily, while women may be satisfied with less sex than that. The longer men go without sex, the more desperate they become for it. The longer women go without sex, the more they don't need it. Find a good compromise and make every effort to follow through, even though one or both of you may be busy and tired. Couples who said they were sexually fulfilled had sex an average of 2.5 times a week.

Regardless of what stimulates and stirs your sexual engine, the reality is that every marriage counselor in the world will agree that intimacy and intercourse go hand in hand. Sex must happen on a regular basis. Plan for it. Prepare your mind for it. Do it.

Consider what the Bible says in 1 Corinthians 7:3–5:

> The husband should fulfill his marital duty to his wife, and likewise the wife to her husband. The wife's body does not belong to her alone but also to her husband. In the same way, the husband's body does not belong to him alone but also to his wife. Do not deprive each other except by mutual consent and for a time, so that you may devote yourselves to prayer. Then come together again so that Satan will not tempt you because of your lack of self-control.

As a married couple, you are biblically mandated to participate in the intimacy-building act of sex. If you don't, the message is clear: Satan is going to get between the two of you and do his level best to split you apart.

What Wives Can Do

Guys are driven by what they see. When they see something they like, the male brain releases a measure of dopamine that makes them feel pleasure. When they feel that pleasure, they remember what caused the feeling and return to it, becoming loyal to it over time.

With that in mind, wives, it doesn't hurt to put in a little extra effort to look nice for your hubby. Sometimes even a small change can make a big impact. Resist the urge to put on ratty sweats as soon as you get home, wear a cute outfit instead of frumpy jeans for a night out, and actually wear some of the sexy lingerie you bought. Also you may need to make the commitment to exercise several times a week, which can, in turn, inspire your husband.

Life happens—aging, pregnancy, illness, weight gain. You're not going to look the way you did when you first met your husband. Fortunately, in deepening love, looks on the outside are less important.

What Husbands Can Do

Guys, the same thing goes for you. A wife can become disillusioned with a husband who lets himself go. Though women are not nearly as sexually driven by sight or appearance as men, a woman still needs to be attracted to her man, and that attraction is created by quality time, caring acts, gifts, words of encouragement, and physical touch. Small efforts such as these nurture a marriage.

Communicate Love Clearly

Every person hears "I love you" in a different way. According to Gary Chapman in his book *The Five Love Languages*, couples need to hear love in the way they understand it most clearly. Quality time, physical touch, gifts, words of kindness, and acts of service are the five ways to express love, according to Chapman. For each individual some ways speak louder than others.

When you identify your partner's love language, you can then communicate "I love you" clearly.

When you identify your partner's love language, you can then communicate "I love you" clearly. A breakdown occurs when you think you're communicating love but it sounds like a foreign language to your spouse, so work hard at discovering your spouse's love language and communicating love clearly . . . and often.

Forgive

Every relationship is going to have an occasional bump in the road, but don't let that bump turn into a mountain by refusing to forgive a mistake. Remember what Jesus said just after teaching us the Lord's Prayer: "If you forgive men when they sin against you, your heavenly Father will also forgive you. But if you do not forgive men their sins, your Father will not forgive your sins" (Matt. 6:14–15). You need to forgive because you need to be forgiven.

Remember that forgiveness is not a synonym for justifying, accepting, or condoning sinful behavior; it is about allowing room for growth and trusting that a change in behavior follows every apology.

Many times couples can let too much time pass without asking for or offering forgiveness. When this happens, bitterness, resentment, and disillusionment set in. Soon the person harboring unforgiveness can start to think these issues wouldn't happen in a different relationship, a deception that leads to a "grass is greener" mentality. Invest in your relationship by asking for and offering forgiveness whenever it is needed.

Keep Learning

Couples who are engaged in learning can continue to grow together with strong bonds. Below are some books that focus on keeping the fire alive.

Chapman, Gary. *The Five Love Languages: The Secret to Love That Lasts.* 2nd ed. Chicago: Northfield Publishing, 1995.

Leman, Kevin. *Sheet Music: Uncovering the Secrets of Sexual Intimacy in Marriage.* Wheaton: Tyndale, 2003.

Thomas, Gary. *Sacred Marriage.* Grand Rapids: Zondervan, 2002.

Wheat, Ed, and Gaye Wheat. *Intended for Pleasure: Sex Technique and Sexual Fulfillment in Christian Marriage.* 3rd ed. Grand Rapids: Revell, 1997.

Growing together and nurturing your marriage is a lifelong task that both husband and wife must undertake. Even in the midst of a culture charged with sexual imagery, your marriage *can* remain healthy and strong if you are vigilant about protecting it.

A Safe Family

What Parents Can Do to Porn-Proof Their Home

I've spent my ministry years in Southern California, Michigan, and currently in Las Vegas. Now that I live in Vegas, I admit I have concerns about what my kids will be exposed to. Despite the parameters we have set around our marriage and our home, a seductive and sensual cloud hovers over this desert town.

Some people have questioned my discernment. "How can you have a ministry to porn stars with kids in your home?" And before I can formulate an answer, they have usually moved on to some other form of criticism of my life. It comes with the territory of what I do.

But you don't have to live in Las Vegas to have your home hijacked by the sex industry. Unless you actively work against them, slowly and ever so subtly, the terrorizing forces that debilitate families, ravage marriages, and hold the soul hostage will set up camp in your living room.

Lurking behind every screen in your home is a portal of devastating potential. Whether through the television or internet, billions of dollars are made annually off the millions of people drawn to sexually explicit material on cable television and the world wide web. On-demand pornography is only a couple of buttons or keystrokes away.

A computer or a television is only a tool; you are responsible for how it's used.

But let's face it, blaming the internet or television for porn addiction is like blaming a pencil for a misspelled word. A computer or a television is only a tool; you are responsible for how it's used. And the fact is: if they have the curiosity, your kids probably know how to use the tools you have in your home to find porn.

The World of Today's Teenagers

Many parents are oblivious to what their children know, often taking a "believe the best" approach with their adolescent child's understanding or curiosity about sex, and crossing their fingers and hoping everything turns out okay. But chances are, if your child is in middle school, he or she has already heard dark and depraved explanations and descriptions of sex.

As I have spoken across the country, I've talked to many kids, and the things they're telling me are beyond alarming. The emails sent to XXXchurch each day confirm it: the age of a child's first exposure to illicit material has dropped rapidly in the last four years.

In 2004 a team from our ministry traveled the country speaking at conferences and conventions. As thousands of kids heard our team talk, many of them returned home and sent us an email asking how to get help. When we could attach an age to the email, we got a general sense of the level of involvement kids of varying ages had with sexual intercourse and porn.

Fast-forward to the summer of 2008, when we're still on the road, still receiving emails. However, now they're from twelve-year-old kids, asking questions that would have made a sixteen-year-old blush only a few years ago. What I learned in the middle school years, my kids will learn before fourth grade.

Our children are experiencing too much too soon.

Consider Lexy's story. We don't know how old Lexy is, exactly, but we could tell from the way she wrote that she was definitely on the younger side of her teens. Lexy sent us an email because, as she explained, she had no one to talk to, and though we have never met her face-to-face, we exchanged a series of emails with her, doing our best to answer her questions.

In her first message to us, she wrote:

X3,
I wanted 2 write 2 ask a srius ?
Cant ask ne1 else. 2 cls 2 me
: (! Had sex in xit hole with my bf
Am I stl a virgn?
LXY

Let me translate her textography.

Dear Craig and the team at XXXchurch.

I wanted to write to you and ask a serious question. I don't feel close enough or trusting enough to ask my parents or my youth pastor. I am sad. I had anal sex with my boyfriend and want to know if I am still a virgin.

Scared and Confused,

Lexy

Obviously, there are so many things that concerned us about Lexy. Her ignorance was staggering—she was more worried about her virginity than about participating in high-risk sexual behavior. It's mystifying how her priorities got so mixed up, and yet there she was, a young woman, asking about behavior in text speak.

Unfortunately, Lexy is not alone. The youth of our culture are being plunged headlong into sexual exposure, usually whether they want it or not. Technology has changed, amplifying the sexploitation of kids. They are able to have instant access to porn, even amateur porn created among peers.

Sexting is a recent phenomenon sweeping the globe, where kids use the camera on their cell phone to take a risqué picture of themselves or someone else and send it via text message to a friend—instant porn. And porn that has left their control and can never be retrieved. Further complicating this behavior, students usually have no idea they have just broken the law, because in many cases they have become child pornographers.

An alarming story was recently reported by CBS News:

One summer night in 2007, a pair of 13-year-old northeastern Pennsylvania girls decided to strip down to their skivvies to beat the heat. As Marissa Miller talked on the phone and Grace

Kelly flashed a peace sign, a third girl took a candid shot of the teens in their white bras. It was harmless, innocent fun, the teens say.

But the picture somehow wound up on classmates' cell phones, and a prosecutor has threatened to charge Miller and Kelly with child pornography or open lewdness unless they participate in a five-week after-school program followed by probation.

Sexting is a recent phenomenon sweeping the globe, where kids use the camera on their cell phone to take a risqué picture of themselves or someone else and send it via text message to a friend—instant porn.

On Wednesday, the American Civil Liberties Union asked a federal judge to block Wyoming County District Attorney George Skumanick Jr. from filing charges, saying that the teens didn't consent to having the picture distributed, and that in any event the image is not pornography.

Called "sexting" when it's done by cell phone, teenagers' habit of sending sexually suggestive photos of themselves and others to one another is a nationwide problem that has confounded parents, school administrators and law enforcement officials.

Prosecutors in a number of states, including Pennsylvania, Connecticut, North Dakota, Ohio, Utah, Vermont, Virginia and Wisconsin, have tried to put a stop to it by charging teens who send and receive the pictures.[1]

Think your kids are safe from this type of behavior? They're good kids who have even promised to remain pure? A study performed by Yale and Columbia universities has shown that youth in organized religious groups who signed virginity pledges like those of the True Love Waits campaign are statistically just as likely to get STDs as those who didn't sign a pledge and are actually *more* likely to experiment with nonvaginal sexual activity, like oral and anal sex.[2]

But the point of all this is that often our children go places where they will connect and communicate with others who may not value purity in the way they should, and no one is immune. Sex is a major topic of conversation at every Christian school, private school, youth group, and locker room— the only difference being the depth of the conversation and the possibility that kids in a Christian school have had some instruction concerning God's expectation of purity—both online and in real life.

Porn is on every high school campus and in every church group. Yes, *every single one*. It is on students' cell phones and laden in the content of the music they listen to.

But there is hope, if we start changing the way we think about our kids immediately. Parents need to think about how to talk with their kids about sex and what to do about the internet and TV.

How Should I Talk about Sex with My Kids?

Most parents tend to panic when they think about the first time their child is going to ask, "Where do babies come from?" At least I do. This is one of the questions I have been dreading since I learned my wife was first pregnant with our firstborn, Nolan. Though it was years away, I knew someday I would have to sit with Nolan and explain it to him.

As parents, what do we do? How should we have "the talk"? When? Where? And most important, what do we say? How much information is too much? The answers all depend greatly on the maturity of each child, but here are some general guidelines to use when considering the timing of the chat.

Your Kids Know More than You Think

Our media driven, sexually charged society paints a false picture of intimacy, replacing the real thing with infatuation and immediate gratification. Kids see evidence of it in advertisements, movies, TV, and music videos. Because of this, kids are usually first exposed to sex through their friends. They talk about it, laugh about it, fantasize about it. Their information is incomplete so it's mostly distorted. Parents can clear up the myths and misinformation their children are inevitably carrying around. If you are wondering if your kids are ready, they probably are.

Don't be naive, but at the same time, don't jump to conclusions. Investigate. Look for opportunities to talk about sex and teach by asking questions. "What do you think about _____?" is a great way to start a conversation with your kids, as long as you honor and respect their opinions. Remember, we all had a lot of bad ideas when we were kids.

Use Correct Terms

I remember in fourth grade when my friend told me his mom had "the talk" with him. He looked at me and said with a straight face, "My mom says I have a 'twig and berries.'"

The poor kid grew up thinking his masculinity was called a "twig."

Start early. At the appropriate age of each individual child, use the correct terms for the parts of the anatomy. The worst thing is to set a precedent with your kids by ignoring the anatomy or mystifying it by using euphemisms. When we do this, we are subtly communicating the real term is "dirty." When inevitably your child learns the *correct* terminology, the subtle thought will creep into his or her mind: "I wonder what *else* Mom and Dad aren't leveling with me about."

Don't just give them the proper names, but, as appropriate, explain the proper functions as well. Kids are going to be naturally curious, and it's our job as parents to appreciate the curiosity and be honest without being sensational or overly dramatic. So when your four-year-old son comes out of the bathroom with his pants down around his ankles, instead of freaking out and screaming, "Pull up your pants or everyone will see your wee-wee!" you can say, "Son, that's your penis, and you use it to pee, but it's also just for you and not anyone else to see or touch. Please go back in the bathroom and pull up your pants. (And don't forget to wash your hands!)"

Trust the Process

Scripture explains that teaching our children is a process: "Train up a child in the way he should go, even when he is old he will not depart from it" (Prov. 22:6 NASB). With this in mind, Christian parents shouldn't just have "the talk" but have an *ongoing series* of talks. Let your child know you are always ready to discuss any questions he or she might have, and then make sure you follow through. Teaching these delicate life lessons requires a *process* of learning, not a onetime conversation. "These words, which I am commanding you today, shall be on your heart. You shall teach them diligently to your sons and shall talk of them when you sit in your house and when you walk by the way and when you lie down and when you rise up" (Deut. 6:6–7 NASB).

A few years ago I wrote a book called *Questions You Can't Ask Your Mama about Sex*. In it I gave the questions I have been asked by hundreds of teens who wondered about suitable boundaries between them and the opposite sex, what constitutes virginity, their sexual orientation, and many other aspects of sex. It's a safe bet your kids also want to know the answers to these questions.[3]

Like it or not, sex is on your kids' minds, and they want to talk about it. So it's up to you to be a safe place where they can get the straight facts about sex without condescension or embarrassment. If you're embarrassed, they will be too. Consider the study from the University of Alberta that found one in three boys are heavy into porn: "Porn has become a major presence in the lives of youth, and while a majority of teens surveyed said their parents expressed concern about sexual content, that concern has not led to discussion or supervision, and few parents are using available technology to block sexual content."[4]

Questions about sexuality are brewing in the hearts and minds of our children. By using the above guidelines and having an inside scoop on what they're itching to know, you'll be ready when the time comes to give them good information.

Shouldn't I Shelter My Kids?

It's tragic that when parents avoid the topic of sexual purity and place value simply on retaining virginity, teens end up making misguided decisions. I know that many parents have "the talk" simply with the goal of avoiding pregnancy, but that motivation is insufficient. The focus has to be much broader.

Like it or not, sex is on your kids' minds, and they want to talk about it.

Instead of preaching a bunch of "do nots" (do not lose your virginity, do not get pregnant, do not get a girl pregnant), instill in your children a value system that emphasizes delayed gratification. Whether it is about your kid's girlfriend or boyfriend or about porn, he or she must understand that a life guided by values *today* will give the teen a more gratifying, more satisfying life *tomorrow*.

Most girls who engage in sexual activity do so for two reasons:

1. They are looking for some measure of acceptance or affirmation.
2. They believe that by giving up certain boundaries they will be loved.

If all you do is give a list of puritanical dos and don'ts without *reasons* for the rules, you're setting your kids up to rebel. Instead, teach them the values behind the rules so they can apply their own critical thinking to situations and make good decisions when temptation comes. Give them the best information you can for *long-term life planning*, measured out with healthy doses of love, affirmation, and explanation, and they'll be more inclined to do the right thing.

What about the Internet?

Children should have access to the internet, but only a crazy person would hand a loaded gun to a child. The internet can be as dangerous as a loaded gun. A child, adolescent, or teen should not be allowed unfettered access to the internet. After all, many *adults* need limitations on their internet usage.

Here are three keys to help families set healthy parameters to internet access.

Supervise

You don't have to sit and watch over your child's shoulder as he or she surfs the web, but supervision of your child's internet use is essential. Supervision can be as easy as setting up the computer in a public area of the home. If the computer is in an office, the computer screen should be visible from the rest of the room and from the doorway. You can't supervise if you can't see the computer screen.

In some cases supervision takes effort beyond the position of the computer. If your kids use laptops to access the internet wirelessly, put the router or wi-fi access point in your bedroom. When you go to bed, turn off the wireless signal. (You will need to make it clear to your kids that if they need the internet for homework, they will need to do it before your bedtime.)

Implement Filtering and X3 Software

I have already addressed the accountability value of X3. Every parent NEEDS to install Safe Eyes Filter on their computer. Get it at www.x3watch.com. This can help you out in so many ways. A friend of mine has a seven-year-old son who surfs the internet on the family Mac. Sound crazy? It did to me until I learned he has access to only eight preapproved sites. Going outside those eight sites is mechanically impossible.

Avoid Peer-to-Peer Servers

Much online porn is offered via peer-to-peer networks such as Kazaa, Lime Wire, and Bit-torrent. These sites allow users to trade files, pictures, music, porn, video, you name it, without going through the web, using instead an online connection to hook into large storage centers called servers. Then users access a simple program to search servers and download whatever they find with a simple click, bypassing all internet filters and even X3 software.

But all that data has to go somewhere, so keep an eye on your hard drive size so you know how much is being used. Movie files are large files and are not easy to hide if you go looking for them. If this becomes a problem, you can always get rid of the internet.

To assure your kids' safety, you may have to learn a little more about computers than you wanted to, but it's worth it to be able to supervise your kids and keep the insidious influence of porn out of your home.

How to Set the Standard

The best way to teach your children what is good and whole-some is to show them by example. Our kids must see a passion in our lives that doesn't get compromised for a cheap thrill. I want my children to see that intimacy with God is of great value and that seeking anything less than God's best cheapens our life. I show this to them by believing it and living it out in my life.

While researching this book, I landed on a website that quoted the words of celebrated Christian author C. S. Lewis:

> We are half-hearted creatures, fooling about with drink and sex and ambition when infinite joy is offered us, like an ignorant child who wants to go on making mud pies in the slums because he cannot imagine what is meant by the offer of a holiday at the sea. We are far too easily pleased.[5]

We are far too easily pleased. Set the standard for your children so they can see that the payoff works. I want to live in such a way that, when I give my kids a healthy parameter, they don't scoff at me with whispers of "What a joke! What a hypocrite!"

How to Cultivate an Ethic of Openness

Feeling free to say what is needed in a conversation begins small and increases over time. Too often tough conversations feel mechanical and scripted, and sometimes they come across that way, making them seem forced. The best groundwork for open dialogue comes from having it at unexpected times.

Many times, the most productive conversations happen spontaneously, which means you have to be on the lookout for an opportunity to throw out a question or two during a conversation with your children that could lead to their speaking what they really feel. You might talk about a current event, a pop culture issue, a political controversy, or the best or worst part of your child's day. Leave questions open-ended and then *let your child talk*.

Find a way to be patient and don't use the conversation as a time to critique or coach. It's a time to listen, not to preach. So let your child talk. When he or she starts to slow down, ask another question similar to the first one, but maybe with a different angle. Then, again, let the child talk.

Look at the problem of having a clammed-up teen. The moment he or she hears Mom or Dad say, "I think we need to talk," the child runs for the hills—or wants to. Why? Because "I think we need to talk" is usually code for "I, the parent, will do all the talking and you, the child, are expected to listen." When this happens the parent gains no insight into what the teen is thinking, and the teen tends to clam up even more.

During long drives, walks, conversations at the dinner table (with the television *off*), and any time it's just you and your child for a period of time, take advantage of the opportunity to listen to your child and really hear what he or she has to say.

Teenagers place high value on environments they deem safe. When a tough situation is on the horizon, they must feel free to share honestly, without retribution. If they have been punished or shot down in past conversations, they won't be as likely to open up to you about their fears and frustrations. If you've had a hand in making your teen feel that it's unsafe to share his or her thoughts and true feelings, it's never too late to repair the damage and start over.

Consider utilizing "safe zone conversations." If a safe zone conversation is declared by parent or child, either can communicate anything without fear of immediate action (unless imminent physical or some other danger is involved). You have your conversation and then allow twenty-four hours to pass before either of you takes any action.[6]

However you choose to provide it, you must give your children the freedom and security of a safe place to say anything they need to say. They desperately want and need an outlet, someone who will listen to their failures, hurts, and pain.

For additional reading and an in-depth look at the numbers behind porn use among teens, see the resource section at the end of this book and the Parents page under Get Help on XXXchurch.com.

A Safe Workplace

An Introductory Guide
for Employers and Employees

The office was buzzing on a typical Friday afternoon. Most of John's co-workers were wrapping up a week's worth of emails and laying out the schedule for the following week. After twelve years at the company, John enjoyed casual Fridays when loose ends were tied up, off-campus lunch appointments ran long, and everyone wore jeans.

As the company expanded, John was content to remain in his role as a department director. He had a team of six people who reported to him and he made a great salary. In fact, John had just recently told his wife of fifteen years that he could see himself retiring with the company. Granted, only forty-two years old, John was being optimistic, but his thoughts of retirement were a comment on how much he enjoyed his job. He loved the people. He loved the freedom. He loved the flexibility.

But on this casual Friday, listening to the buzz outside his office, it became apparent to John something was not right. He looked out his door and the first person he saw was Drew, the head of information technologies, whose job was to keep all of the company's computers linked together on a server and to keep them connected to the internet. Drew was surrounded by a bevy of workers while he barked orders to his assistants as they took a brief moment at each computer workstation. Initially John was taken aback; usually scheduled maintenance was done on weekends, not on Friday afternoon.

As John watched, he realized the workstation computers were each getting scanned and loaded with an internet filter. Drew made his way over to John's opened office door. "Johnny, can you believe this madness?"

John offered a sheepish shrug and a halfhearted nod. Drew continued, mincing no words. "Who in their right mind would take the chances of surfing that stuff on company time?"

Slowly the pieces of "surfing that stuff" began to stick to John's conscience, and though Drew was a formidable image only inches away, John ignored the rest of his tirade. Instead, John's mind began to rapidly recall all the times he, while tucked away in his office, would slip over to a porn site to sneak a peak.

Occasionally John would see a quick image of a sensuous seductress that really stirred him, so he would grab his portable jump drive and insert it into his computer's USB port. With the clandestine cover-up in progress and portable storage ready to receive, John would download the porn to a folder he slyly called "Trash." He had once seen a movie where hackers hid malicious material in trash folders, because it is the last place an average person would look. He never saw the irony of the name he chose for his stash of porn. And he failed to realize that each of the more than two hundred images in his "Trash" folder could wind up playing a part in his demise at this job.

Drew's words snapped John back to real time.

Nothing done online is anonymous.

"Someone at the company has been surfing porn, and they're going to be nailed." John's stomach sank. He felt as though he was going to faint.

"I just wish people would get it," Drew finished. "Nothing done online is anonymous."

Brazen Use

Porn use at work is now so widespread that just about every company has a monitoring system in place. According to a 2008 Nielsen online study, 25 percent of employees with internet connections use them to visit porn sites, which is up 23 percent from the previous year.[1] A recent survey found that employees spend an average of 1.86 hours per eight-hour workday on something other than their job, not including lunch and scheduled breaks. Based on those averages, employee time-wasting actions cost U.S. employers an estimated 544 billion dollars in lost productivity each year.[2]

More than half (52 percent) of the 2,706 people surveyed admitted that their biggest distraction during work hours is surfing the internet for personal use. For the record, other distractions cited by respondents included socializing with co-workers (26.3 percent), running errands outside the office (7.6 percent), and simply spacing out (6.6 percent).[3]

A national survey of U.S. employees who have internet access at work found that 24 percent said they'd used a company computer for romantic/sexual purposes. Twelve percent said they'd accessed sexual content from a workplace computer, and 12 percent had forwarded sexual content to other employees while at work. Six percent had engaged in sexual instant message sessions while at work, while 10 percent had used an office computer for online dating.[4]

You may feel safe surfing at work, but the truth is, if your company is monitoring your internet access, you're putting yourself and your job at risk.

Some unsuspecting internet users get lulled into a sense of security and confess that, because they have never been warned or gotten caught, they think they are okay. Nothing could be further from the truth. You may feel safe surfing at work, but the truth is, if your company is monitoring your internet access, you're putting yourself and your job at risk. All online traffic, both incoming and outgoing, is monitored, a "firewall" is in place for security purposes, and all traffic is registered. Created to prevent hackers, firewall. logs list all connections and actions.

Here are some reasons you may not have been caught yet: many IT directors don't feel that it is their job to "out" people who violate company policy. Either they have not been empowered to blow the whistle, or the person they have to out is their supervisor or superior. Imagine having to let the cat out of the bag that the CFO is dabbling in porn. They know but aren't telling anybody. Other IT directors and system administrators don't have the time to review individual usage reports.

Each day—or in some cases, each week—reports are run and directed to the administrators, who review them either electronically or manually, looking first for hacking attempts. This is when porn websites that have been visited may be discovered. An accidental discovery of an employee's secret use of porn sites may result in the loss of his or her job.

Porn online is not the only thing to avoid. Spending time on gambling sites, chat rooms, social networking sites like MySpace and Facebook, and blogs unrelated to work content can all be considered a lack of productivity, which is grounds for termination.

Employers and Employees Beware

Nearly a decade ago, in 2001, the Computer Security Institute, in conjunction with the FBI, surveyed corporations and found that 91 percent of their respondents detected employee abuse of internet access privileges, with 74 percent experiencing financial losses totaling an estimated 256 billion dollars. The violations detected? Downloading pornography and pirated software. Social networking and instant messaging were not included in this report.[5]

Some might think that smaller companies would be the only ones violated by porn use, since they have less access to technology, oversight, or updated tracking software compared to their Fortune 500 counterparts. But according to this study, throughout the country, corporation size was irrelevant. Whether the company was big or small, the numbers remained the same across the board.

In 2005 half of all Fortune 500 companies addressed at least one incident over a twelve-month period related to an employee's porn use. In these cases the offenders were fired in 44 percent of cases and disciplined in 41 percent.[6] This means that if you work for a big company and you're checking out porn on the job, you have a 15 percent chance of avoiding detection and an 85 percent chance of being found out. Are you comfortable with those odds?

During a one-month window (March 2006) of testing and tracking, a survey conducted by Comscore found 61 million unique U.S. visitors logged into pornographic websites, with every fifth visitor from an office workstation. In other words, 20 percent of porn use in that month—or 12.2 million people—came from the workplace.[7]

The cost goes beyond lost productivity. Companies are responsible for the viewing habits of their employees when those habits affect other employees. Imagine employee A is watching porn in his cubicle when employee B walks by and sees it. If employee B suffers any residual effects from A's use of porn, litigation becomes a real possibility.

What if the action of the employee becomes overt? If sexual aggression, flirtatious behavior, or even sexual harassment is evident, the company is responsible. Nearly one-third of U.S. Fortune 500 companies have had sexual harassment cases filed against them by employees objecting to their colleagues' internet viewing habits.[8]

John's Choices

John just wanted to run. Paranoia began to creep into his mind. He wondered if Drew already knew. Had Drew been pumping him for information? John began to think of his history with the company; if Drew knew he was a culprit, why hadn't he warned him? Was he out to get him?

Paranoid feelings always accompany a cover-up.

By now Drew had gone back to his crew to wrap up the afternoon installations. Still feeling lightheaded, John slipped behind his desk. Dangling from the USB port on the front of his computer was his jump drive. He thought he had covered his tracks but had failed to consider that the company server was stalking his every keystroke and mouse click.

He faced a dilemma. According to Drew, it sounded like they knew who the culprit(s) were. Should he confess? Thoughts of unemployment were nothing compared to the guilt he was experiencing. He thought about his wife, his children, his church, his role as a board member for the local Little League—he was overwhelmed.

One part of him screamed, *Hunker down and ride it out*— the voice of cover-up. Equally as loud but not nearly as aggressive was a voice that said, *Tell your boss today and your wife tonight*—the voice of character.

John tried to convince himself the company might show him mercy because of his willingness to come forward. Maybe there would be a measure of grace because he had not yet been caught. Or maybe he had already been caught and potentially identified, just not spoken to yet.

By the time John was able to move from behind his desk, it was almost 6:30 p.m. The offices had been vacant for nearly two hours as people had left early to get their weekend started. Not John. He wanted to crawl into a dark hole.

Over the weekend John sat down with his wife and his pastor and confessed it all. He went into detail, explaining the storage cover-up, the bent he had toward the seductive, and how long he'd been living his lie. He explained how deeper issues had plagued him, including an occasional trip to a strip club while away on business and the more than three dozen porn movies hidden in the garage toolbox. He did the right thing and laid it all out for them.

As his wife wept, the pastor referred them to marriage counseling and to XXXchurch for some follow-up and software options. It was shortly after this first meeting that we met John and his wife through a series of emails and the occasional phone call to check in.

John's pastor had no idea how his employer would react, and even our ministry had little experience when it came to handling the fallout from an employer. We told John he would have to be honest but also to expect the worst, knowing he'd violated his role and his employer's trust.

He requested a meeting with the CEO. Waiting for the meeting was excruciating. In the back of John's mind was the thought that he could just ride out the storm and own it if he was ever confronted. We advised him to own it even if he *wasn't* confronted.

Some would argue against our counsel, but we have learned that, with many employers, the cover-up is worse than the crime. Consider if you were an employer, would you not respect the person who in humility comes in and confesses? John might say something like, "Sir, I know that the company computer system has been violated on company time. I have to confess that I am one who has violated it. Over the past two to three years, on occasion, I have surfed pornography while on the clock. I realize this was a breach of trust and the corporate ethics we live by. I am guilty. I have informed my wife and my pastor, and I am willing to accept the consequences of my actions and pay back to the company the equivalent of lost time and productivity, with either my accrued vacation time or cash."

Imagine yourself as an employer—how would you respond to someone who came to you like this? How would your company respond? What does your heart tell you to do? Granted, some of the details must be guided by company policy, but where permitted, if I were an employer, I would want to offer this person an opportunity to keep his job. If he had the courage to admit his guilt to his boss, and if the porn did not violate the law, I'd give a measure of amnesty.

Perhaps the stability of John's job, accountability, and increased oversight from his employer will help keep him on the path to true wholeness. A job can actually be a great tool and motivator to help people like John remain true to their promises to reform.

What Policy Can Employers Use?

A company's human resources department can play a big part in assuring that any and all company policies operate within the limit of the law. In addition to standard operating procedures and employment policies, companies should have a

Companies should have a clear set of standards regarding online computer usage.

clear set of standards regarding online computer usage. Each company differs due to the nature of their business, but vague standards or unwritten expectations will be nearly impossible to apply and enforce.

A company should have written standards concerning the use of the internet for gambling, social networking, or viewing porn, as well as standards for cell phone use.

Gambling

With the advent of online gambling, the standards should include state laws, other legality issues, and company policy. Companies should be consistent and realize the hypocrisy of prohibiting online gambling while permitting a companywide Final Four pool, Super Bowl betting, and the like.

Social Networking Sites

One broad policy on social networking sites may not be sufficient for addressing every circumstance. For instance, there are some company departments where Facebook and MySpace are unacceptable and other departments where they are valuable tools. The finance department for a marketing firm does not need its employees updating their Facebook status every twenty minutes. At the same time, this type of viral movement may be a major initiative for a design or branding team. Companies must write policies that take into account different needs.

A Porn Policy

A company should clearly define its expectations when it comes to porn use. All employees should know that the company computers are monitored and reviewed and that viewing porn could be grounds for immediate termination. Any illegal activity is grounds for immediate termination and investigation, and child pornography puts the entire company under legal scrutiny.

Cell Phone Use

With today's technology, the internet can be accessed by either a personal or company-issued cell phone, and many porn cases have involved mobile phones. Employees need to know that the company reserves the right at any time to call in and scan for content cell phones that belong to the company. Cell phone policies should include usage minutes for online time, text messaging, chatting, and surfing the web. Many hours are wasted when people text on company time. A text string lasting throughout the day, even if it's void of sexual content, still defeats productivity.

John Comes Clean

A week had passed with no meeting scheduled, and John had to get his confession off his chest, so he decided to poke his head into the office of Bob, his company's CEO. As John stood before his boss, voice quavering with nervous tension, angst filled the room. John cleared his throat. "Bob, can we sit for a moment?" Before his boss could answer, John continued, "I have some devastating news."

John sat down and laid out a full disclosure to his stunned boss. Over the next hour John untangled the web of deception he'd sewn together on company time, and by the end of the conversation, John was once again broken both by the mess he'd made and by the humility that comes with confession to the right people. The longer John talked, the more he realized Bob had had no idea of his transgression. But it didn't matter. It felt good to come clean.

Bob gave no immediate response to the way John's admission would affect his job. As CEO he had learned to reserve all comments until the completion of his own independent inquiry. However, because of John's willingness to sit and explain his behavior with such vulnerability, Bob assured him that if what he had said was true, despite the disappointment, the company would promise confidentiality and continued employment.

John knew that everything he had said was true, that his was an even deeper confession than any software report could generate. On that day, nearly three years ago, John found freedom.

What about You?

Are you an employer? How will you respond if an employee comes to you and confesses viewing porn on company time?

Are you an employee? Do you view porn sites at work? Will you make any changes in your behavior? Take this chapter as a warning to stop today. You don't necessarily have to be like John and confess to the boss, but you can start living honorably from now on. Be thankful you have not been caught. Consider this grace. If you've been living a lie at work, at least confess to your spouse or accountability partner, then pray for wisdom on how to proceed with your employer.

Maybe porn is not your problem, but you spend company time on surfing the web or chatting on Facebook. Do you need to start working a full day and putting in all the time you are paid for? It's up to you.

Be faithful.

Be honorable.

Be honest.

And remember: the cover-up is always worse than the crime.

Seeking Help

What to Do If You
or Someone You Know Is in Trouble

Do you have a problem and need help? Does someone you know need help? What should the wife of an unfaithful husband do? What should a pastor do if he is struggling or if someone in his congregation or a fellow staff member is entangled in porn? Whether it's in the workplace or the family, in marriage or in ministry, where can a person turn for help, for hope?

For a man or woman who is just now beginning to recognize there is a problem, the first steps in seeking help can be very difficult and at the same time incredibly liberating.

Accountability

The greatest tool we can offer those who want to find freedom from the use of pornography is strong accountability. This means you allow someone in your world, whom you respect and trust, to examine the darkest crevices of your life through questions. You welcome scrutiny to keep you from stumbling. If you know someone is going to ask you where you've been online, you're less likely to go where you shouldn't go. Accountability is a biblical mandate that is used to examine the human motive and bridle that which is unacceptable. "As iron sharpens iron, so one man sharpens another" (Prov. 27:17). Author J. Hampton Keathley III puts it like this:

> Man is a rebel who wants to do his own thing without any or very little accountability for his actions. Since the fall of man, this has been the case, but a worldwide phenomenon of our day is a defiance of any form of established authority whether religious or secular, social or political. When God either does not exist in the beliefs of men or when the truth about God is distorted into man's own image of who and what God is like, everything is permitted, morally speaking.[1]

By letting someone else into your life, into the deepest, darkest corners where all your junk is hidden, you will find the freedom that comes from complete honesty and openness. This is the essence of accountability, an active way of living out this truth: no one can succeed in this life on his or her own.

But just having an accountability friend isn't a guarantee of success. Many people with accountability still fail to find freedom for two very different reasons.

1. People fail because they refuse to *listen* to their accountability friend, the person who has offered his or her time, energy, and honesty to ask the questions no one else will

ask. Perhaps the accountability relationship was established out of emotion, or worse, guilt. Let's say you had a failure, and in an attempt to maintain damage control and through your quasicontrition, you established a weekly meeting with a friend. There is no benefit to enlisting the trust and confidence of a loyal friend and then ignoring that person's questions, comments, or concerns. When we think we don't need to listen to the advice of our accountability friend, we're setting ourselves up to fail.

This is the essence of accountability, an active way of living out this truth: no one can succeed in this life on his or her own.

2. Accountability fails when the accountability partner, while good-hearted, lacks the courage and strength to keep the addicted person honest. In reality this is probably the reason the particular person was chosen. Some people just don't want to be accountable, so they choose a partner who will not ask the tough questions.

Unfortunately, accountability isn't something that can be thrust into a person's life. You and I can't go to someone and say, "You are going to be accountable to me." That never works. The desire for accountability has to originate in the heart of the person who *really* wants to change.

When we developed X3watch software, some criticized us for not just offering a filtering system, but we felt that would be shortsighted. Filters are valuable, and we definitely recommend them, but they are never 100 percent accurate and can often be overridden or sidestepped. Accountability is a choice and can be very effective when people agree to be accountable to someone else. We believe, however, it is not an issue of either/or but instead, both/and. Both filtering and accountability are necessary, and both should be used.

The desire for accountability has to originate in the heart of the person who really *wants to change.*

We created a number of websites where multiple levels of accountability are available. First, www.x3watch.com is a site where the X3watch Accountability Software is available for free. In addition, a filter service called Safe Eyes is being offered with this book (you can preview it at www.x3watch.com). These two tools—accountability and filtering—work in concert for a higher level of internet safety. And despite the fact that we recently celebrated our one millionth download of X3 Watch, we have a lot of work to do—porn's reach is far too extensive to stop now.

Richard's Story

While sitting in an airport, I took a call from Richard, a pastor in Washington State. He is an associate pastor at a large, nondenominational church near the Oregon border. He is quick-witted, has a brilliant mind, and is a sterling example of what the second-in-command should be. Richard has no illusions of grandeur and does not want to be the lead guy; he is there simply to help navigate the daily pitfalls a church faces. And he had a problem.

Their church had undergone a severe porn issue with the discovery of two pastors on their support staff using church computers to access porn. The issue of online safety had dominated recent staff meetings.

Richard had sat tensely through the latest meeting, knowing that accountability software was a must. He was ready to suggest it as an option. The lead pastor began to discuss how they planned to curtail the unwanted behavior by offering "high-level accountability" filtering throughout the organization.

Wanting to offer solutions as part of his role in the leadership, Richard interjected his opinion, describing the need for the accountability to be accessible to everyone, even those in the congregation, and explaining in detail how the X3 software works.

Richard knew the software works. Online agencies, tech magazines, ministries, and churches have all reviewed it, with the best explanation coming from AssociatedContent.com:

> For all [intents and] purposes, it's a snitch to your family or accountability partners. Whenever you browse to a website on the internet which might contain some questionable material, X3 will make a note of the website, save it to a hidden file, and will email two people who you choose the list of suspected questionable websites at the end of the month. They state the information is "meant to encourage open and honest conversation between friends and help us all be more accountable." . . . it is very effective for Christian Men who have accountability partners. It might not stop every instance, but men will be a lot more hesitant to go to those websites knowing that their buddy will know about it as well.[2]

As a man who has eyes, I often find myself in the shadow of Paul the apostle, who once wrote, "I am the chief sinner" (see 1 Tim. 1:15). I think of King David, who failed miserably with his voyeuristic and adulterous tendencies (see 2 Sam. 11–12). If these two biblical giants were susceptible to failure like everyone else, then I am no different. If you think you are immune, then there is a much bigger problem in your heart than porn.

Regardless, I have yet to hear a logical defense as to why X3 is not viable, especially when used in conjunction with a strong filter. Our email in-box is filled each week with people from every walk of life who say "X3 Accountability is the best!" I always become suspect when I am told that a person refuses to load the software. You can imagine why.

As Richard finished his push for the software, the staff in the room became a microcosm of the greater body of Christ. Each person had listened to the explanation through his or her own filter, instantly forming opinions on the way it would affect his or her life, good or bad.

The lead pastor responded, and Richard was blown away by what he said. "X3 Accountability won't work!"

The pastor declared that a filter would be the best option, because it prevents porn viewing ability rather than simply reporting it to an accountability partner.

But with the internet growing daily and new porn sites added by the hour, a filtering company has trouble keeping up with the tricks, misdirection, and URL hijacking the porn industry has mastered.

A filter by itself can offer a false sense of security that surfing is safe. The reality is that a lock keeps out only the honest person, while a thief finds a way around it. A person longing for porn will find their way around a filter, and when they do, no one will know.

Without someone else "up in your business," a person, even a pastor, can be trapped with a conflict of interest. There are many pastors who feel as if they can't fail, and if they do, they can't let anyone know for fear of losing their job. We hear it often. Pastors need help.

A lock keeps out only the honest person, while a thief finds a way around it.

"We will filter every church computer, including mine!" the lead pastor announced.

To see that the job was done right, the pastor went to each staff computer and loaded the newest version of a filtering system himself. But here's why Richard called me. He was there when the pastor installed the filter on his own computer, and he was there when the pastor entered the override password to turn off the filter. The pastor did not want people to load X3watch and was also the only person who had password override ability for the filtering program. Richard has never suspected or accused his pastor of indiscretions, but this is very dangerous ground. When someone holds the power and avoids the process for himself, that's a big warning sign.

At the time of this writing, the situation in Richard's church is still the same, but Richard knows that in the future he may need to change jobs and move to a place where the pastor leads by example and welcomes online scrutiny.

Traits That Tell the Story

After nearly ten years in the porn-help business, and having heard thousands of stories, we have identified the following five traits as the most prevalent indicators of a porn problem.

1. Deceiving Those around You

The vortex in which porn addiction exists is deception, and people who are ensnared by porn will lie to cover up their tracks. Trying desperately to hide their porn use, they create cover-ups, like clearing the cache folder and emptying the temporary internet files folder, hoping not to be discovered. From the dads who hide their stash to the moms who rendezvous with other desperate housewives, people will lie about the lies that they lie about.

2. Living in Fantasyland

The seductive nature of porn acts like a magnet, drawing the user into a world of airbrushed bombshells and fabricated scenarios. The actresses offer images that are far from reality—aggressive nymphs who stop at nothing while sexually consuming an average Joe. Their tanned bodies never say no, are never tired, and are willing to explore without hesitation. At the climax, they yelp, scream, and orgasm to the top of their lungs, all the while saying, "You're the best and biggest." This, of course, is sheer fantasy.

When the DVD is over, the next encounter with one's spouse will pale in comparison. Fantasy has eclipsed the real world.

Expectations about sex and intimacy have been distorted; they are unreal and can't be maintained in a real relationship. Somewhere along the line, the porn user forgets that the people in the video are acting.

3. Adjusting One's Perception of Beauty

Guys, the competition on the screen has made it tough for your spouse to measure up. Because she is playing soccer mom, chef, taxi driver, and housemaid, she is not able to do endless hours of fitness training, capped with an appointment at the tanning salon. Instead, she wears sweats and spends her spare time balancing the checkbook. Fantasy alters one's perception of beauty, making healthy marital arousal impossible.

4. Lagging Sex Life

Using porn can cause sexual desire to slacken, and mild impotence can create a mental and emotional disconnect. Intimacy is gone, and the wonder of the marriage bed is extinct. Resentment builds toward your spouse because she won't perform like actresses in the porn flick.

5. Antisocial Behavior

Overwhelming guilt can cause antisocial behavior, and isolation becomes soothing. Users tend to spend more time with pornography than with people, and this pattern becomes the perfect sin-management tool. They can indulge their addiction and no one knows about it. When they are alone, their love is for their laptop. Silence is seductive, a reminder that no one is home.

This can be a particular snare for the single person, who is often alone and may fear never finding a lifetime partner. This combination can drive his or her attraction to fantasy. *If I never get married, at least I have porn*, the single addict may reason—empty words from an empty heart.

Stories of Healing

As if the five above traits weren't enough, I feel compelled to mention one more. Inevitably porn will stop doing the trick, and when this happens, most addicts venture out into the real world to add a human touch to their addiction. From hooking up with a prostitute to engaging in an affair, the cost of porn use will continue to escalate. We see it happen all the time.

Many porn users will read this and not give it a second thought, thinking, *Not me!*

We understand. Just give it time. There are many people having unprotected sex with strangers or indulging in criminal behavior who never imagined they would do what they are doing.

Maybe even now you are engaging in behavior that is out of control and are wondering if it's possible to turn yourself around. In the midst of broken families and broken people, the good news is many do find freedom and wholeness. This is an email we received from someone who had just gone through our X3pure program:

Thank you so much for helping me fully understand what I've been dealing with. For most of my life I've tried to control my thoughts and actions on my own (I've had help here and there but was never completely honest with all the issues I was going through) and I would always get discouraged when I would completely fail. I came to a point . . . where I was like, "You know what? I'm sick and tired of living a double life and not getting others involved in my issues." I now meet twice a week with my pastor and an accountability partner. That has helped me in more ways than I ever knew. I haven't had the urge to masturbate in over a month now and through this program and my mentors I've been able to get more effective tools in combating my problems. Now this isn't to say that I haven't had thoughts that keep popping back into my mind all the time, but now I'm prepared to fight them with Scriptures and prayer and get my mentors involved in my struggle. Before this program I hadn't fully understood what I was doing. I knew it was wrong and I knew it wasn't helping my relationships with my girlfriend (soon to be fiancée), family, and friends. Now I know where I'm weakest and I know that even if I stumble and fall I must not let that get me down and try to make me give up, I know that it's a constant battle and it's something I'll probably have to fight to the grave. . . . From one lost person who was living a double life before: THANK YOU.

Here's another email. We received this one from "Josh." I hope you find it as encouraging as we do:

Today was the day. It finally happened. My wife discovered my dirty "little" secret.

She called me on my cell phone and confronted me about the internet files she found in the History on my web browser.

What could I do? I was caught. The crazy thing is I tried to lie to cover it up because I was ashamed and embarrassed. She told me not to come home that night and she began to cry and weep like I have never known before. It started with an e-mail I received and that spark ignited a wildfire that I have been trying to hide. I was curious and let it consume me.

She cried and said she felt like killing herself and she cursed me out and hung the phone up. I broke spiritually at that moment. I desperately tried to call her back and after the third time she answered the phone, still crying. I dropped to my knees in public and sobbed uncontrollably, I thought my wife, the woman I love—the woman I know without doubt God brought into my life, I thought she had killed herself. I didn't want to live anymore. I figured it didn't matter because I already felt dead on the inside. I'm trying really hard not to cry as I write this.

I begged her to let me come home. The silence on the phone seemed like an eternity. And the drive home was even longer. I felt the Holy Spirit compel me to ask for forgiveness. I refused—I didn't think God would this time. I mean, I think I have abused 1 John 1:9 beyond the limit. I felt compelled again and muttered out a prayer of repentance. My wife didn't know how to handle it. We are a young couple, who've never had any real challenges—certainly nothing on this level.

When I got home, she sobbed uncontrollably again and locked herself in our bathroom. She couldn't look at me. After 30 minutes, she came out, sat down, and asked, "How long? How long has it been going on?"

I confessed everything and tried to tell her how much I love her and how I didn't mean to hurt her and cause her pain. She told me she still loved me and I broke out in tears. I thought porn had ruined my marriage. We talked until 2 AM and she forgave me. I told her not to say it unless she meant it, but she held me and told me it was true. I told her how sorry I was and she said we'll get through it. And then she dropped a bomb on me:

She asked me to forgive her for watching porn too!

She had been looking at porn sites (straight ones) in secret, but it wasn't a struggle for her. I was floored. We both had dirty little secrets and it almost killed our marriage. She cried because the Holy Spirit confronted her about the "splinter" in her eye while she was confronting me about the 2 x 4 in mine.

We held each other for over 2 hours and let the Holy Spirit minister to us and our marriage. We made a promise to be more honest with each other and openly talk about struggles we are facing instead of finding "alternatives" to cope with feelings and emotions. The word says, "You shall know the truth and the truth shall make you free." I know the truth . . . and I am glad to say that I am free.

Thank you, XXXchurch.com, you are a bright light in a dark world. Thank you . . .

One who is forgiven,
Josh

Change

A change awaits the heart that is willing. Consider what is at stake. Look at and read through these emails of encouragement. Take inventory.

The best is yet to come . . . if you will allow it.

The Porn Industry

An Unlikely Mission Field

One of the things we do at XXXchurch is go to porn shows and hand out Bibles with covers that proclaim: "Jesus Loves Porn Stars." For the most part, people are supportive. Rarely have I been anxious about being at one of these shows—except for the time when Donny showed up.

Donny hated us. In his mind we were Public Enemy #1.

You may remember Donny from chapter 2, the pastor's kid who got so burned by Christians that he became a porn producer. While he was in college, he began to create porn through an amateur site, shooting pictures of "college-aged girls next door." Large companies including *Penthouse*, *Playboy*, and *Hustler* saw his work and employed him, and he was on the fast track to success in the industry. He had money, sex, and an increasing appetite for power, but with these perks came a broken internal compass.

That's when he saw us at the porn shows, standing off to the side, watching us at the booths, waiting to catch us doing something illicit. When we stayed faithful to both God and our spouses, it made him even angrier. At first, he thought we were perverted pastors just trying to get near the porn industry in the name of ministry. Or maybe we were peddling our wares for the same reason everyone else was there—to make money. Or maybe we had some kind of kinky religious site.

As Donny watched us over time, he eventually saw that XXXchurch was making a difference. In fact our message was familiar to him, since we were communicating some of the same things about love, hope, and forgiveness he had heard his dad proclaim from the pulpit years ago. At the bottom of his heart, he knew something in his life had to change but he still ignored his inner voice. He sought ways to argue, fight, and discredit us.

But he couldn't.

Donny battled us for over a year and to this day he remains the only person we have ever banned from a discussion board. Yet God reached him.

Donny had just left Sacramento after signing the most lucrative deal of his producing career. He was driving home to Redding when God showed up in his car. Near the outskirts of town, Donny broke down and began sobbing.

What was going on with him? He was confused; it wasn't supposed to be this way. He was supposed to be celebrating the new cash, not crying in conviction. Why all these tears? Why couldn't he stop them?

He knew. Within moments he called our office, and within days we were at his home in California.

As a ministry, we decided it was our responsibility to invest in his future, so Donny Pauling, the former porn producer, is now in seminary studying to be a pastor. When we think of his journey, we know God is at the center of his restoration and we are thankful to be a part of it. But does Donny's turnaround make right what had gone so horribly wrong? We are very glad that Donny is doing well, but the collateral damage of his past haunts him still. The industry won't allow it to go away. It just won't.

He gets emails like these all the time:

Hey, Donny,

I have a HUGE problem. I'm getting married in a month, and my fiancé FOUND MY PICTURES on the internet. He is beside himself. He is hurt and shocked and being that we are supposed to tie the knot in less than a month, I'm freakin suicidal!!! Freakin sick over this. . . . throwing up, cannot sleep at all . . . I never thought in a million years that would ever happen. How long do those pictures circulate?? I am seriously pissed.

I know I did those pics and yes it was my fault, I want to get them OFF the internet. Is there any way possible to do that ASAP? I will pay you the money back, whatever it takes. This will and is ruining my life. I am fearful that his friends will see and torture him about it, or the people I work with in the military (they are all men). I am absolutely SICK over this. I can't eat or sleep and I honestly don't know what to do. I swear to you, I never thought this would happen. I mean, there are a million girls on the freakin internet. . . . why me?! and because you are supposed to be a changed man? into God and everything? please . . . I need to know that you understand my situation, and find it in your heart to help me. This is destroying me. I know I am 100% responsible for taking the pictures, it's my fault. But it was a long time ago, and I was single and I needed the money. But isn't there anything you can do to please help me now??? This was like 2 or 3 years ago? Why are my pics still on the damned internet?

My military career and soon to be marriage (if he still will) is riding on this. Don't my pictures expire after a certain time? and you just put new ones up? or sell new ones to companies to flush out old girls? I think you can read the desperation in this email.

I am completely desperate (again) at this point Donny and need your help. Can you help me? Please. I need EVERYTHING removed. What can we do? I'll pay you money, anything. PLEASE say you can help me. PLEASE.

The pain and desperation in her writing are the two vice grips that clamp Donny's heart. Though God has forgiven him for all of his past failures, the results and the fallout of his rebellion are still floating in cyberspace. Sadly, there is no way to retrieve these images, no way to erase this part of his or her past. What's done is done.

The Porn Pastor and the Porn King

A few years ago a porn industry publication listed the top fifty adult film stars of all time. Ron Jeremy was happy to be at the top of the chart. It is not that he's the most attractive guy; he got started by posing for *Playgirl* because he was notably endowed. But beyond that, he's very average. Guys can relate to his average looks and portly body.

A few years ago Ron was walking the floor of the Adult Video News trade show in Vegas, when he passed the XXXchurch promotional display. He stopped and chuckled. A "Jesus Loves Porn Stars" banner hung behind the table, and I stood there with a team handing out Bibles. I had been there for a couple of the previous years but wasn't aware that Ron knew who we were.

As Ron stood and signed autographs, he began to smirk, giggling and looking in our direction. He approached me and we got to talking. He thought I was a bit crazy to think that porn was harmful, but he respected my thoughts. He also respected the fact that I was willing to show up at a place that most men of the cloth, as Ron calls them, would condemn to hell.

A few months later I was invited to go on a college campus to debate the effects of porn. I called Ron to see if he wanted to do it, the "porn pastor" debating the "porn king." Ron is always up for a good debate, so he took the gig, thinking at least it would be a great gimmick or PR stunt—not to mention he would be well paid.

The debate was successful, which led to another and then to another, and to continue the story in Ron's words: "What began as a single debate has evolved into more accurately a dialogue. Craig is not trying to convert me to some church and I am not trying to get him laid. I respect his wife and family and after getting to know him think he's a good guy.

"We both agree that what makes a great country is that he can speak his mind on his beliefs and I can still make porn. Both are expressions and both rely on free speech. Traveling with Craig and seeing his family has made me think of things. I make him think. We get into it. The debate spreads into the backstage area, the bus, the restaurants, radio interviews, and

TV shows. He has introduced me to his friends and I have introduced him to mine."

I have seen a dark side of the industry that is miles away from painted faces and airbrushed fantasies.

He is a porn star. I am a pastor. But it is through this strange friendship that I have learned about the industry in a very direct way. I have seen a dark side of the industry that is miles away from painted faces and airbrushed fantasies. Though Ron is my friend, I can't say it strongly enough: the sex industry destroys lives.

A Values Vacuum

After traveling across the country and seeing different sides of Ron, I see he is not the snapshot of the sex industry that most see. He is fun to be around and amicable. Though he has very strong opinions about porn, its production, and its supposedly harmless nature, he is also willing to listen. Many of my encounters with Ron are representative of encounters with so many other people I have met, like Jimmy D, a porn producer who offered to make a commercial for XXXchurch, or the endless string of performers we've talked to and helped. Each person has his or her own reason for being in the sex industry.

Some have used porn to feed their own addictions: sex, drugs, attention, publicity, or a combination of them all. Others have a strong desire to please people—even if it means dehumanizing themselves. Porn devalues the performers, turns them into objects of gratification. They are like cigarettes, smoked and then thrown away.

I remember being told of a scene on a porn set "Angie" was asked to perform. She resisted and asked not to have to do a particularly humiliating act. Cajoled and convinced to do it, or rather extorted and threatened with a loss of pay, she gave in. As the producer yelled "Action," she began to absorb sexual abuse and degradation for minutes that seemed like hours. The cameraman moved in for a better angle on the money shot.

When the producer yelled "Cut," Angie quickly rushed off camera and vomited into a nearby trash can. When the gut-wrenching convulsions finally subsided, weakened and still nude, she walked off the stage, lay down like a toddler, and sucked her thumb. It doesn't take a psychologist to identify what was going on: she was reverting back to a time of innocence. The vomiting, the pain, the regression—the value of her self-worth had been ripped from her.

But the next scene had to be shot, so moments later she had to get back into position and begin to act as if she was loving what she was doing. Over and over Angie performed, each take dehumanizing her a little more. Each shot taking another piece of her soul.

Consumers never see this side of it, and producers generally aren't concerned with what happens when the camera is *not* rolling, as long as they get their shots when it is.

Sure, we acknowledge that Angie was on a set shooting a certain type of porn. But had there not been a demand for that type of porn, she would not have been there. Stephen, a staffer at XXXchurch, said it best in one of our staff meetings. "You want to stop looking at porn? Go to a porn show."

It sounds like a paradox. Why would anyone go to a porn show to stop looking at porn? In the right circumstances with the XXXchurch team behind you, going to a porn show can help people like Stephen view women in the show as real people—people with hopes and hurts just like anyone else. Stephen's first porn shows illustrated to him how real these men and women are, how valuable they are to God, and how the industry has messed with them.

Unfortunately, the industry trap works as a feedback loop that draws people in. The endless roller coaster of porn is as seductive for the performer as it is for the user. Many in porn want out; they just don't know how to get out. Outside the industry they can't keep the same revenue flow. In many cases they have built a career without having any educational or job aptitude. They don't know what to do with their lives. Lack of a clear purpose that extends beyond making money is one of the greatest problems for people in the industry. Visionless, directionless, and rudderless, they drift aimlessly into deeper dependence on others, into depression, and into chemical addiction.

What can they do? Where can they go? Who will help them?

At XXXchurch, we are committed to helping those who want out of the industry, and we assist them with accountability.

Sin City: The Industry Defined

The more we have learned about pornography, the more widespread we have found the problem to be, so we packed up our

Midwest offices and moved from Michigan to the heart of the industry, Las Vegas. We discovered an industry that is complex and multilayered, where one group depends on another and vice versa. Producers depend on performers. Performers depend on purchasers. Purchasers depend on production, which is what is pumped into the hotel rooms via television and the internet. It is a multifaceted problem with no easy solutions.

But what exactly is "the industry"? We use the term for any revenue-making venture that uses sex to make a profit.

Porn

The subcategories of porn can be broken into many groups, but the reality is there are three major segments: internet, film, and print.

INTERNET PORN

As the new kid on the block, the internet has made porn consumption convenient. With a high-speed connection and the click of a mouse in the privacy of your own home or office, you can access the vilest content instantly. The biggest concern for internet porn producers is to determine whether it should be given away free or for a fee. Most sites are free, with revenues made by banner ads and click-through links. The more traffic the site receives, the more money the website can demand from ad sales.

FILM

The old porn theaters have mostly gone away, with the exception of a few in seedy neighborhoods. What used to be available only on old 8mm reels is now sold and packaged on DVD, thousands of which are produced each month. Producing and duplicating a DVD requires very little up-front money, while a ton can be made on the global market.

PRINT

Print magazines such as *Playboy* and *Penthouse* continue to thrive, and so do their online and DVD spin-offs.

Prostitution

Prostitution is the oldest profession in the world and one that takes very little talent. We have observed four different kinds.

HOOKERS

The street corners of many inner-city areas are filled with hookers, so-called "women of the night," though the profession is no longer limited to women. Today HIV/AIDS and other sexually transmitted diseases are so prevalent on the streets that having sex with these men and women is like playing Russian roulette, while vice cops and undercover operatives continue to try to sweep the streets of them. Most hookers are "managed" by a ruthless man called a pimp who sees them, not as women, but as moneymaking property.

ESCORTS

An escort is a more discreet, higher-priced prostitute than the hooker on the street. In Vegas escorts advertise on billboards and in the yellow pages, and sometimes, though they're usually paid to accompany a person to an event, inevitably, sex will be the larger expectation. Many are booked through an agency—just another version of the street hookers' pimp system.

BROTHELS

On the outskirts of Las Vegas are *legal* houses where women work their room. Men and women come to broker a deal, money is paid for a negotiated time, and the sex act is performed. The world-famous Mustang Ranch is the most notable brothel, though sometimes these brothels are nothing more than double- or single-wide trailers.

COVER OPERATIONS

Massage parlors and motels are just a few of the cover operations for prostitution, where the business in the front is just a facade for the "party" taking place in the back. Cities lacking control over these operations have also had recent increases in human trafficking issues.

Strippers

Strippers are women and men who dance nude or nearly nude for cash and tips. In many states, if alcohol is being served, women are allowed only to go topless. Though they don't explicitly perform sex, the degradation of being ogled is just as detrimental to their soul. Strippers generally operate in three different arenas: strip clubs, juice bars, and private parties.

Strip Clubs

Depending on the city and its ordinances, dancers at strip clubs can offer private "lap dances" to paying clients. Many strip clubs are covers for prostitution rings.

Juice Bars

In many states, such as California, the juice bar is a strip club without the alcohol. These establishments that serve non-alcoholic beverages are allowed to show full nudity.

Private Parties

Order a stripper for a private party and that person decides how far is too far. It depends on the conscience and conviction of the stripper what he or she will do behind closed doors.

The Consumer

Together these different soul-consuming professions, which make a business of sex, make up the industry. They all represent a product that is in demand. Within the heart of humankind, since the breakdown in the Garden of Eden, is a drive for illicit sexual experiences. Consumers drive the market; if there were no market, it would all go away. Instead, entrepreneurs representing the erotic create, develop, nurture, promote, sell, and profit from humankind's sin nature.

Whether it is being patronized in a corner market, a seedy back alley, a motel room rented for an hour, or on a laptop, the industry would inevitably go bankrupt without the consumer. Instead, with a market that increases daily, sex is a multibillion-dollar-a-year industry. It has created a pandemic of epic proportions.

The vortex of seduction pulls in people seeking money, fame, and sometimes sex, and they become the performers. It pulls in people seeking a sexual experience, and they become the consumer. Both groups are bottom-feeders who hover on the lowest rung of the sex industry, yet they are the reason the industry is so lucrative.

From Pain to Promise

The sounds of sobbing seemed to scream through my phone. On the other end of the line was my new friend Chris. At the age of twenty-eight, Chris had already learned about the dead-end destination of the industry. He had come to a realization that porn takes people farther than they want to go, costs them more than they want to pay, and keeps them longer than they want to stay.

Porn takes people farther than they want to go, costs them more than they want to pay, and keeps them longer than they want to stay.

As a gay man needing some extra cash, Chris originally sought out some innocent modeling jobs, but within weeks the cash was flowing and his alter ego "Pete" had been created.

Fast-forward three years and thousands of gay sex scenes later, and Chris was emotionally devastated. Used up physically and empty spiritually, he self-indulgently searched Google for the words "Pete + Porn," possibly hoping his popularity would make him feel better. But on this night, instead of an illicit image, he discovered a XXXchurch outreach, our "Pete the Porno Puppet" commercial, made for us by porn producer Jimmy D. It's about keeping porn away from children. Intrigued and curious, he watched the puppet clip and thought it was the craziest thing he had ever seen. But then he decided to search around XXXchurch.com and found hope as he read about lives being changed through X3watch, "Jesus Loves Porn Stars" Bibles, and outreaches to people who sought to leave the porn industry.

He sent us this email: "I hated myself. I hated porn. I had absolutely no joy in my life. My entire existence was a sham. I maintained a blog and I fabricated a healthy and happy persona, while behind closed doors I spent the majority of my life hidden with shades drawn, lights off, crying most of the night, sleeping most of the day. I remembered a time that I was happy. I used to have such a thirst for life. Now, during my darkest times, I secretly wish it was all over. I feel worthless, dirty, ashamed, despondent, ugly, and tired. I feel like I have lost any semblance of what I used to be. The only thing that keeps me from doing something stupid is my family. My mom and dad would be devastated."

I found out where Chris lived and connected him with a pastor friend nearby. After they had spent hours on the phone together, the local pastor made two promises. First, Chris would be welcome at their church and God would be there. Second, Chris would anonymously be able to discover a new love in God. The pastor made good on his promises.

With a new lease on life, infused with hope, and having been forgiven for his past, Chris found at XXXchurch practical tools to make a healthy transition back into reality. These solutions, financial support, health care, and solid counseling, stabilized and sustained Chris. Now he's thriving with a new sense of purpose and destiny.

Escaping from Porn Prison

Heather

Heather Veitch was born out of wedlock to a seventeen-year-old mother and was never given a chance to make anything out of her life. Growing up poor and surrounded by drugs and crime, the world came at her too fast, too soon, and by the age of sixteen she had been raped twice. Lacking hope and feeling that the bad things in her life were her fault, she denied sex to no one.

Now, at seventeen, like her mother, she too was pregnant. Needing cash and without any structure or moral insights, she started dancing, then stripping.

The sex industry offered a steady flow of cash that just didn't satisfy. In time, Heather found herself sitting in a church and hearing a message of hope in Jesus. She learned that Jesus could reach her despite her baggage. In that moment Christ's love became real to her, and over time she began to find in church a community where she could grow spiritually.

Years passed and her faith in God grew, as did her desire to fulfill his call on her life. With a passion to use her pain to help others find purpose in life, Heather began to minister to people stuck in the industry. She had not known of others who were trying to reach them but then, through a variety of avenues, she discovered XXXchurch. She could not believe we too were reaching people who were making porn and helping people who were watching porn.

Inspired by our story, Heather started a national ministry to women in the porn industry. JC Girls (Jesus Christ Girls) is now affecting and helping women see the porn industry for the dead end it is.

Julie

Julie left porn on June 20, 2007. In just two months she walked away from the enslavement of the porn industry, stopped smoking pot, found a new place to live, and got a new full-time job that offers full benefits. It's amazing how her life has turned around.

Julie came from a violent childhood and her family moved around a lot. She began stripping at a young age, which ultimately led her to acting in porn movies. Porn shattered her life, and after diving into drugs to help deaden the pain, she eventually decided she wanted out.

When we met Julie, we saw in her a gifted person, so we committed to helping her leave the industry. Now our ministry friend Shelley Lubben meets with her and is committed to helping her maximize her gifts. Julie is creative, and we hope to see her enroll in vocational school to increase her opportunities to use her creativity.

Julie wants to use her life story to help others. Most girls who escape porn want to fade into obscurity, but Julie wants to go public, determined to help others learn the truth about porn.

With a five-year-old daughter who doesn't live with her, Julie has realized she needs to be a mom to her princess, hoping that, in time, because of the steps she has taken, she and her daughter will be reunited. She is determined to help her child avoid falling into the porn trap that ensnared her.

Becca

Becca shoved the needle into her arm and, as the heroin flowed into her bloodstream, hit rock bottom. After only eighteen months in the industry, she was already burned out and used up, so she contacted XXXchurch with the hope of escaping, and God began to restore her in amazing ways.

Knowledge of God was not new to Becca—her father was a pastor, and she had attended Christian school as a kid. But like Donny Pauling, she'd been hurt and disillusioned by the ugly side of religion. Even so, now she knew it was time to come back. Seeking a mentor and someone who was confident that a transition from porn was even possible, Becca contacted Shelley Lubben and started on her road to recovery.

Now in school to design websites, Becca says she trusts in God to provide for her. "Life is sweet now!" she recently told us.

Tanya

Tanya contacted us originally as her alter ego Jersey, coming across our path through MySpace. Tanya spoke about many sad things in her life, from her father's sexual abuse to the abuse she endured performing in porn. If one word could define Tanya's life, it would be *abuse*. Today Tanya wants to please God and fulfill the purpose he has for her life. Truly for Tanya, old things have passed away, and all things have become new.

Bobby

Porn star Bobby was once married to a porn queen and had a life many men envy, though they would have no idea what Bobby and Brianna's life together was really like. With more sex and women than he could handle, Bobby said it was all in the name of employment. In the midst of his "stellar" porn career, Bobby's world began to unravel.

Having crossed paths with XXXchurch, Bobby began to see how empty the patterns of his life were leaving him, especially as his marriage began to unravel and ultimately crash.

With few authentic places to turn, Bobby looked to God. Now his heart is changing and softening, and he's beginning to imagine what life can be. He has left the industry and has been completely faithful to severing his ties to porn, though many people he cares about are still in the industry. Now Bobby knows Christ must be first in his life. In time he hopes others will see the validity of his chosen path.

Hope for Anyone

We continue to be amazed at the number of people leaving the industry. In 2006 and 2007 we helped more people leave the porn industry than in all the previous years of our ministry combined. Our work is paying off.

We have a mandate. We are committed to showing the way to true life to those who have been held hostage by the porn industry, and the only thing that can slow us down is lack of the resources we need to keep up with the demand.

To those who have escaped, all of us at XXXchurch applaud you and honor God. He has done and will continue to do a good work in you.

We believe hope is available to everyone in the industry—if they are given a chance. The common thread that holds each of these stories together is God's ability to reach people where they are and bring real change to their lives. Through a network of people committed to addressing the porn industry with love, XXXchurch will continue its mission, but we can't do it without help.

The common thread that holds each of these stories together is God's ability to reach people where they are and bring real change to their lives.

You can be part of the change. Consider the following:

Is there any access point in your home where the porn industry has slipped in?

Have you contributed to the fiscal gains of the industry?

In the last seven days, have you violated your eyes with explicit material in any form?

Have you told the truth on the previous three questions?

What practical steps could amputate and cauterize the effects of the industry in your world?

What would happen if those who are Christ-followers abstained from the wares of the industry?

Imagine the impact on the supply side of porn's economic flow if Christians committed and adhered to Scripture's mandate to "meditate on that which is pure" (see Phil. 4:8)!

1. What if we really believed the Bible is true when it tells us: "Your eyes will never be satisfied" (Prov. 27:20 NKJV).
2. What if we treated an affair of the mind and heart with as much seriousness and avoidance as a physical affair?

Is it possible to abstain from all this? Of course! God would never ask us to do something he hasn't given us strength to accomplish.

The way we answer could literally change the world.

Beating the Porn Pandemic

Being on the road takes its toll on our team. Traveling thousands of miles each year wears on the family and on the soul. Rolling into any given town, we are faced with the prospect of being either embraced by the community or looked at with skepticism. Most of the time, churches, organizations, and individuals are excited to hear what we have to say.

Woven into each of our talks are stories of hope, many of which we've included in this book. Yet these stories are only half the message. The other half is the need to have a practical plan in place to help remedy the problem of porn use before it gets out of control.

Steps Everyone Can Take

The following is our list of the top ten easy steps you can take to beat the porn pandemic. And rather than offering a list of things you *can't* do, our list is equipped with valuable tools where we encourage and equip you with the things you *can* do to keep your life pure. Every reader, regardless of age, gender, or income level, can do these. There is not a cost to any of them, so money (or lack of it) can't be an excuse. Most can be incorporated into our everyday lives, so time can't be an excuse.

Commit yourself to the following and communicate your commitment to those closest to you.

1. Go Online Where Others Can See

The first and perhaps most important thing you can do to curb a desire to dabble in porn is simply to put your computer in a public place. With the option of a mobile/wi-fi service, any room in the house can be a home office. But such great convenience also requires great responsibility.

> *The first and perhaps most important thing you can do to curb a desire to dabble in porn is simply to put your computer in a public place.*

Make a commitment to use your computer in a public place. If it's a desktop computer, place it in a well-trafficked area of your home. If your decor demands it be in an office, make sure the desk is situated so that anyone in the room can see the screen. Many companies have gone to this policy for office setup. It prevents users from easily browsing porn out of sight of people passing by their office.

Keep your home office door open. We have heard hundreds of stories of spouses who walked into a room when the door had been closed, only to find porn on the computer screen.

Conversely, I have yet to hear a single story of a person being caught using porn when he was using the computer in a public place where all could see the screen. In short, surf publicly.

2. Load X3watch Accountability Software

We created the X3watch software to offer accountability to all computer users, to give you a safeguard against going where you should not go. This software provides accountability through a partner—someone of your choosing—who receives an email every couple of weeks that will list any questionable sites you have visited during that time span. If a link does appear, this does not automatically mean the site is porn; it just gives the accountability partner a heads-up. (For example, say you are surfing for a men's soccer coed league. The words *men's* and *coed* trigger that site to show up, but it is not a porn site.)

3. Keep Your Spouse in the Loop

Don't fall into the trap of thinking porn or outside erotica can help enhance your relationship with your spouse. It won't; it will only damage it. Instead, remember the best way to increase the love and vitality of your relationship is close, intimate communication. Seeking deeper intimacy means allowing your spouse to connect in *every* area of your life. By allowing him or her to know about your successes and your failures—even though it may be very difficult for your spouse to see the failures—you cultivate an atmosphere of authenticity. Talk about both the ups and downs in your life. This will keep your relationship growing and vital.

You may want to consider allowing your spouse to receive one of your accountability emails when using the X3watch software.

4. Use Positive Visual Triggers

One practical way to help maintain healthy parameters is to have positive visual triggers in place as reminders to do the right thing. Surround your office or computer area with pictures of family and friends. Use a family photo as the desktop wallpaper on your monitor. Also images that remind you of your faith can motivate you to live a life of purity.

Don't fall into the trap of thinking porn or outside erotica can help enhance your relationship with your spouse.

5. Remember the Real Story behind the Porn

Each person who appears in porn has a story. Behind every image of porn is pain, conscious or not, and the sooner we can begin embracing the people of porn as just that—people, human beings—the sooner we can beat the porn pandemic.

6. Talk about It

We travel and speak at presentations called "Porn Sunday" at churches around the country. Conservative denominational churches and independent churches have asked us to be part of their Sunday gatherings, all in an effort to communicate the harmful and long-term effects of pornography.

We have been able to share the stories of so many and put a face on the pain and derailment of people in porn. We talk about it, raising awareness, and we tell success stories of those who have been freed from porn, so others are able to see hope and find healing. You never know when your personal story will help someone else, so don't be afraid to share what God has done in your life.

7. Bring Resources to Others

We have seen many lock arms with us and join our team in bringing resources to everyone in need of help in this area. Those who partner with XXXchurch have the opportunity to minister life and love to those who want to free their lives of porn, as well as to help walk people out of the porn industry. Much can be accomplished when we participate in practical expressions that show God's love and kindness to *all* his children.

8. If You Mess Up, Own It

I've written it before: "The cover-up is worse than the crime." Should you experience failure in this area of your life, be quick to acknowledge it to God and to your accountability friend. This type of ownership cultivates humility and prevents pride and the need for lies. Once this is done, move on with a conscious commitment and take practical steps that will help you steer clear of making the same mistake twice.

9. Have a Purpose for Being Online

We talk to so many people who did not set out to get hooked on porn. Many people have explained to us that it occurred through a combination of curiosity and idle time online. They went online with no purpose. It's easy to accidentally get into a porn site while surfing the web without any real purpose or destination in mind.

Inevitably, over time, the thought occurs, *I wonder if I can find this online*? Within a few Google inquiries, viewers are staring at a vast array of seedy content. One look stimulates a release of brain chemicals that will make you want to look again. If you aren't online for a reason, log off and spend time with your family, read a book, or go to bed.

10. Remember, There Is Help

For those who are wrestling with the web, there is help. We suggest the thirty-day purity process called X3pure, an online workshop that helps Christians begin the recovery process. It provides a plan of attack and a road map for recovery. It can also be a huge help to your spouse. You can sample it at www.x3pure.com. Also our two new books, *Pure Eyes* for men and *Pure Heart* for women, will help you with practical insight for maintaining sexual purity.

Many people have successfully found a path back to purity, and you can too. These ten steps are practical and simple. They are meant to jump-start your road to recovery.

Ways Your Church Can Help

For the church to navigate through the minefields of porn usage, it has to demonstrate a commitment to character and integrity and avoid compromise. We've partnered with hundreds of churches to help people on both sides of the industry. Here's how your church can become a light in the dark world of porn.

Acknowledge the Problem

Acknowledging the problem is essential. Too many churches are silent and unwilling to dialogue about this addiction that affects so many. Every church must begin the conversation among its parishioners. If the illness is never diagnosed, a cure is impossible. Will it get messy? Will there be some fallout? Of course. However, *real* bad news is better than *fake* good news. Talking about this in the open is better than hiding it.

To help churches acknowledge the problem of porn, we created a number of events and provide everything a pastor needs to get the conversation started.

PORN AND PANCAKES

Men's breakfasts are nothing new and are a perfect place to have a gut-level talk on porn. Most men enter such a discussion guarded and leave challenged. Sometimes former porn producer Donny Pauling is able to take part in a Q & A session. Donny is an expert at letting men know how the porn world has mastered the art of luring men.

Visit www.pornandpancakes.com.

Porn and Pastries

Similar to Porn and Pancakes for men, Porn and Pastries is for women only. Wives tell us how the Pastries events offer a real look at what they had suspected for years was destroying their home. Occasionally we receive a follow-up email from a woman explaining how her marriage was spared because after one of our events her husband admitted to porn use, and they are now walking toward redeemed love.

Our purpose for starting the Porn and Pastries events was to help women deal with their husband's problem. To our surprise women started to tell us their own stories of addiction, so often the event ministers to women who want to end their use of porn.

Visit www.pornandpastries.com.

Porn Sundays

When churches are willing to deal with porn, help and hope for those who are trapped become more feasible. Some churches want only the Pancakes and/or Pastries events. But when we can do both Sunday morning and Sunday evening presentations, the entire church can be educated, equipped, and empowered to get beyond the dirty little secret so many in both the secular and sacred worlds are hiding.

Porn Sunday is a turnkey event. A comprehensive interactive manual, video support, speakers, small group materials, and other resources are available for any church to hold the event. With endorsements from churches of all sizes and across denominational lines, XXXchurch communicates the hard-hitting truth of how families are being destroyed.

I'm committed to maintaining these events, and I always want to leave a church in a good position to address the issues. Our host churches have seen firsthand that awareness can bring change. We launched a website, www.pornsunday.com, to tell these firsthand stories of transformation.

These events are excellent ways to stimulate the dialogue among men and women in the church and make it no longer taboo to say "porn" within the walls of the church. As awareness spreads, pastors can talk about the value this honest discussion adds to their church's spiritual formation. Hurting people are able to start taking the necessary steps to get free and find wholeness.

Visit www.pornsunday.com.

Create an Atmosphere of Authenticity

An increased level of awareness by acknowledging the big elephant trouncing through the church lobby is an essential stepping-stone toward strength. It's great to hear that fifty men stood at a men's breakfast and disclosed their pain from porn, but if the atmosphere has not been conditioned with authenticity, those fifty men will feel alone, abandoned, and regretful that they were honest.

Authentic environments speak acceptance, so that, despite a person's issue, struggle, or problem, he or she still feels loved. Authenticity demands that who I *say* I am matches who I *actually* am, but if a person feels he will be attacked or ignored for his vulnerability, he will not be authentic.

Creating an authentic atmosphere can be difficult. Those in leadership positions must lead by example and be willing to be vulnerable. I am not suggesting you make up something—that's actually the worst form of fraud. Instead, lead a discussion with something like this (in your own words, of course): "Today I want us to reflect on the value of who we are and what we believe. I want us to leave today with confidence that our behavior matches our beliefs. There are times when my behavior does not match my belief. I believe that God can do all things. But sometimes, even as a leader, I do not feel strong enough, smart enough, or even successful enough to accomplish what I need to do. Have you ever felt this way?"

Once someone admits to a problem with porn, *listen.* Don't bow to the internal pressure to try to keep adding additional insights or, God forbid, to *fix* the person.

An atmosphere that has been charged with authenticity won't come overnight. Rather than setting out to change your community in one meeting, start with a single conversation. An authentic conversation continuing over time with any faith group will lead to an authentic culture, and when the culture is changed, every person seeking a greater depth to his or her interpersonal relationships will find hope.

In an attempt to move in this direction, churches have started hosting the events I described above, and in many of these churches, men and women have heard the significance that came from the authenticity and found their first steps to freedom from the porn pandemic.

Offer and Apply Amnesty

Sometimes I learn a ton about God through being a dad. I remember a time when my four-year-old daughter came to me telling me she messed up. We had told her over and over again not to use her crayons on the wall, and she'd just done it again, just colored a masterpiece in the forbidden zone. It wasn't that I didn't like the picture; it was just done in the wrong place.

Authentic environments speak acceptance, so that, despite a person's issue, struggle, or problem, he or she still feels loved.

Most people who engage in porn do so for the pleasure they receive from it. God is not against pleasure, but the pleasure must come from the right stimulus in the right context. When a husband is stimulated by his wife, God delights in the couple's pleasure; when the same pleasure is created outside of marriage or with the wrong stimulus, it is displeasing to God.

I liked the picture my daughter colored—just not on the wall. But something occurred to me when she proactively came to me and admitted she had not done things right. As her father, I had to honor the fact that she owned her fault. I knew it was a teachable moment, and everything inside me pushed me to explain, offer, and then grant amnesty because of her honesty.

If congregations or faith communities do not offer a measure of amnesty when people are honest, the fear of coming clean will outweigh the courage it takes to make the move. Scripture is strong. Consider this passage from Proverbs 28:13: "He who conceals his transgressions will not prosper, but he who confesses and forsakes them will find compassion" (NASB).

I wonder how many people want desperately to make things right but feel as though they can't because they are aware of the environment of judgment and punitive retribution.

I wonder how many people slipped deeper into debauchery because, when the time was right for them to own it, they had no place to go and no person in whom they could confide.

What would happen if churches and their congregations made a hard assessment of what is really going on in the pews? What would the church of today look like tomorrow if we really began to pursue honor, humility, character, and consistency?

How would *acknowledging* the problem of porn take shape in the community where you are involved? Has a facade been built that prevents honesty? Is it possible that the cover-up is worse than the crime? What would an *authentic conversation* about real-life struggles look like in your church? Would it sound real or foreign to the churchgoer's ear?

The Individual's Responsibility

Have you ever *experienced amnesty* or relational grace? What did that do to your commitment to the person who offered it? Have you ever *offered amnesty* to someone else? If some of the people we've mentioned in this book walked into your world, could you offer them grace? Would you be willing to look beyond a person's career in porn to develop a relationship with him or her?

If change is to happen, it's up to you. You and your church must make the choice to recognize the porn pandemic and take preventive steps immediately. You can help keep your family, your church, and yourself pure by understanding the seriousness of this pandemic and taking protective steps against it.

Appendix

Statistical Data on Youth and Internet Pornography

Following are excerpts and synopses from studies on internet porn use among youth.

An anonymous survey of over 400 students aged 13 and 14 in rural and urban Alberta, Canada, schools revealed these statistics:

Boys aged 13 and 14 living in rural areas are the most likely of their age group to access pornography. . . .

A majority of the students, 74 percent, reported viewing pornography on the internet. Forty-one percent saw it on video or DVD and 57 percent reported seeing it on a specialty TV channel.

The study also revealed . . . boys doing the majority of deliberate viewing, and a significant minority planning social time around viewing porn with male friends.

Sonya Thompson, author of the study, urges parents to raise their level of awareness and set boundaries for and open dialogue with their children about this harmful and pervasive influence. "It needs to be talked about," she says. "There's a whole subculture we are not addressing."

Sonya Thompson, "Study Shows 1 in 3 Boys Heavy Porn Users," University of Alberta, March 5, 2007; http://www.healthnews-stat.com/?id=450&keys=porn-rural-teens

- - - - - - - - - - - - - - - -

A 2005 survey of 1,500 youth internet users ages 10 to 17 revealed that nearly half (42 percent) of the users had been exposed to online pornography in the previous year. Two-thirds (66 percent) of those exposed reported their exposure was "unwanted"; one-third (34 percent) was "wanted" or a mix of wanted and unwanted.

The proportion of wanted exposure for boys increased from 1 percent of 10- to 11-year-olds to over one-third (38 percent) of 16- to 17-year-olds, who reported intentionally visiting X-rated sites in the past year. Wanted exposure among girls was significantly lower across the board, beginning at around 2 to 5 percent for ages 10 to 15 and ending at 8 percent for ages 16 to 17. The study also noted that "44% of youth with wanted exposure said they had gone to X-rated sites on purpose when they were 'with friends or other kids.'"

Unwanted exposure, starting at 17 percent in the boys' youngest age bracket, also increased with age, to over one-third. Girls' unwanted exposure began at 16 percent in the lowest age bracket—significantly higher than the boys'—but increased to the same percentage (34 percent) as the boys' in the highest age bracket. These findings were up from 25 percent in a similar survey conducted in 1999 and 2000.

The highest risk activity for both unwanted and wanted exposure was using file-sharing programs to download images.

- -

Exposure also resulted from stumbling onto X-rated images or sites through other normal internet use, including talking online with friends, playing games, and visiting chat rooms. The study advises, "It is also important to note that not all unwanted exposure incidents were unintentional. In 21% of incidents, youth said they knew sites were X-rated before they entered the sites."

Although not completely effective, filtering and blocking software reduced the risk of unwanted exposure, as did attending an internet safety presentation by law enforcement personnel.

The study concludes with a call to action:

> Medical practitioners, educators, other youth workers, and parents should assume that most boys of high school age who use the Internet have some degree of exposure to online pornography, as do many girls. One clear implication is that professionals should not shy away from this topic. Frank direct conversations with youth that address the possible influences of pornography on sexual behavior, attitudes about sex, and relationships are needed.

Janis Wolak, Kimberly Mitchell, and David Finkelhor, "Unwanted and Wanted Exposure to Online Pornography in a National Sample of Youth Internet Users," *Pediatrics* 119, no. 2 (2007): 119, 247–57; http://pediatrics.aappublications.org/cgi/reprint/119/2/247

– – – – – – – – – – – – – –

The second *Youth Internet Safety Survey*, conducted in 2005, found that

> approximately one third of youth Internet users (34%) had an unwanted exposure to sexual material in the past year, an increase from 25% in *YSS-1* [*Youth Internet Safety Survey*

1999–2000] that occurred despite increases in the number of families using filtering, blocking, or monitoring software.

Of these unwanted exposures, 79 percent occurred at home; 9 percent at school; 5 percent at friends' homes; and 5 percent in other places, including libraries. Approximately 29 percent occurred while with friends or acquaintances.

Janis Wolak, Kimberly Mitchell, and David Finkelhor, *Online Victimization of Youth: Five Years Later*, Crimes Against Children Research Center, University of New Hampshire (2006); http://www.unh.edu/ccrc/pdf/CV138.pdf

– – – – – – – – – – – – – – –

In a New Zealand Internal Affairs study of over 200 child pornography offenders, the largest single age group was young people ages 15 to 19; over half of all offenders were under 30.

Caroline Sullivan, "Internet Traders of Child Pornography: Profiling Research," New Zealand's Department of Internal Affairs, October 2005; www.dia.govt.nz

– – – – – – – – – – – – – – –

Over 70 million people visit porn sites each week; about 11 million of them are under the age of 18.

"Protecting Kids Online," *Washington Post*, July 1, 2004; http://www.washingtonpost.com/wp-dyn/articles/A19307-2004Jun30.html

– – – – – – – – – – – – – – –

In a study of sexual solicitation of internet youth users, the sender of the solicitation was unknown to the youth in over 90 percent of the cases. Almost two-thirds of the unwanted exposures were delivered to addresses used solely by the youth. Once the pornographic site is accessed,

[they] are often programmed to make them difficult to exit. In fact, in some sites the exit buttons take some viewers into other sexually explicit sites. In 26% of unwanted exposure incidents, youths reported that they were brought to other sex sites when they tried to exit the sites they were in.

Janet Mullings et al., ed., *The Victimization of Children: Emerging Issues* (Binghamton, NY: Haworth Maltreatment and Trauma Press, 2004)

- - - - - - - - - - - - - -

When installed at moderate settings, pornography-blocking software minimally affected access to sexual and reproductive health information while blocking 90 percent of pornographic content.

C. R. Richardson et al., "Does Pornography-Blocking Software Block Access to Health Information?" *Journal of the American Medical Association* 288, no. 22 (2002): 2887–94; http://jama.ama-assn.org/cgi/content/short/288/22/2887

- - - - - - - - - - - - - -

Most children between ages 8 and 16 have viewed pornography on the Internet. In many cases, these sites were accessed unintentionally when performing an innocent search, often in the process of doing homework.

London School of Economics, January 2002

- - - - - - - - - - - - - -

In 2006, $3.62 billion was spent on video porn sales and rentals, as compared with $2.84 on internet pornography. The porn industry's revenue is larger than the top ten technology companies combined: Microsoft, Google, Amazon, eBay, Yahoo!, Apple, Netflix, and EarthLink.

Jerry Ropelato, "Internet Pornography Statistics," Internet Filter Review; http://internet-filter-review.top tenreviews.com/internet-pornography-statistics-pg2.html

- - - - - - - - - - - - - - -

Easy access to sexual imagery could be the catalyst behind the rise of sex attacks committed by children. A 2007 article in the *London Evening Standard* cites alarming statistics:

The number of cases in which children received court orders or warnings for sex offences has jumped by 20 per cent from 1,664 in 2002/03 to 1,988 last year.

"Web Is Blamed for 20 Per Cent Leap in Sex Attacks by Children," *London Evening Standard*, March 3, 2007; http:// www.thisislondon.co.uk/news/article-23387540-web-is-blamed-for-20-per-cent-leap-in-sex-attacks-by-children.do

- - - - - - - - - - - - - - -

In a 2007 Cox Communications internet survey among young people aged 13 to 17, the following findings were posted:

A majority (58%) said they do not think posting personal information and photos on public networking sites is unsafe.

Fully 47% said they are not worried about other people using their personal online information in ways they don't want them to (down from 57% in '06).

An alarming percentage of teens reported they post information online about the city where they live (58%) and the name of their school (49%). Percentages were significantly higher among older teens (70% and 64%, respectively).

Nearly two-thirds (64%) post photos or videos of themselves. Girls and older teens, in particular, said they have uploaded personal pictures to the Internet.

Nearly one in 10 teens (8%) have posted their cell phone number.

"Research Findings: 2007," Cox Communications Teen Internet Safety Survey, Wave II; http://www.cox.com/take Charge/includes/docs/survey_results_2007.pdf

– – – – – – – – – – – – – – –

While many teens are taking precautions in obvious areas of online risks, those with online profiles are generally more likely to post their first name, their photo, and the name of their hometown and school; one quarter include their email and last name.

Some 32% of online teenagers (and 43% of social-networking teens) have been contacted online by complete strangers and 17% of online teens (31% of social-networking teens) have "friends" on their social network profile who they have never personally met.

More parents are monitoring their children's online activity, using both technical and nontechnical means, including filtering and monitoring software, checking internet history, and placing the computer in a public area.

Amanda Menhart and Mary Madden, "Teens, Privacy, and Online Social Networks," Pew Internet and American Life Project; http://www.pewinternet.org/Reports/2007/ Teens-Privacy-and-Online-Social-Networks.aspx?r=1

Notes

Chapter 1 Pornified World

1. Lee Rainwater, *Social Problems and Public Policy: Deviance and Liberty* (Hawthorne, NY: Aldine Transaction, 1974), 143; http://en.wikipedia.org/wiki/President%27s_Commission_on_Obscenity_and_Pornography.

2. Roger Ebert, "Inside Deep Throat" (11 February 2005); http://rogerebert.suntimes.com/apps/pbcs.dll/article?AID=/20050210/REVIEWS/50128001/1023.

3. "Are There Lessons to Be Learned from Porn Sites?" *Knowledge@Wharton* (9 May 2001); http://knowledge.wharton.upenn.edu/article.cfm?articleid=354.

4. Ibid.

5. Jerry Ropelato, "Internet Pornography Statistics"; http://internet-filter-review.toptenreviews.com/internet-pornography-statistics.html.

6. Michael Kirk and Peter J. Boyer, "American Porn," *Frontline*, WGBH Educational Foundation, aired 7 February 2002, available online at http://www.pbs.org/wgbh/pages/frontline/shows/porn/view/?utm_campaign=viewpage&utm_medium=viewsearch&utm_source=viewsearch.

7. Emmanuele Richard, "The Perils of Covering Porn," *A USC Annenberg Online Journalism Review*, posted 3 April 2002 and modified 5 June 2002; http://www.ojr.org/ojr/business/1017866651.php.

8. *Frontline* interview with Dennis McAlpine, PBS, August 2001; http://www.pbs.org/wgbh/pages/frontline/shows/porn/interviews/mcalpine.html.

Chapter 2 Pornified Church

1. The Barna Group, "A Biblical Worldview Has a Radical Effect on a Person's Life" (1 December 2003); http://www.barna.org/barna-update/article/5-barna-update/131-a-biblical-worldview-has-a-radical-effect-on-a-persons-life.

2. "ChristiaNet Poll Finds That Evangelicals Are Addicted to Porn," Market Wire press release (7 August 2006); http://www.marketwire.com/press-release/Christianet-Inc-703951.html.

3. Ramona Richards, "Dirty Little Secret: Men Aren't the Only Ones Lured by Internet Porn: A Revealing Look at the Shameful Addictions of a Rising Number of Christian Women," *Today's Christian Woman*, September/October 2003; http://www.accessmylibrary.com/coms2/summary_0286-797871_ITM.

4. Ibid.

5. "Ted Haggard's Letter to New Life Church," *Colorado Springs Gazette*, 5 November 2006.

6. "Disgraced Pastor Haggard Admits Second Relationship with Man," CNN.com (30 January 2009); http://www.cnn.com/2009/US/01/29/lkl.ted.haggard/.

7. Richard Niolon, PhD, "Defenses" (December 1999); http://www.psychpage.com/learning/library/counseling/defenses.html.

8. "Mormon Church-Owned Paper Rips Romney on Porn," *World Net Daily*, 13 July 2007; http://www.worldnetdaily.com/index.php?fa=PAGE.view&pageId=42565.

Chapter 3 Honorable Men

1. See Genesis 3:6–7.
2. See Genesis 9:20–21.
3. See 2 Samuel 11:2–5.
4. See Romans 7:21–24.

Chapter 4 Feminine Wholeness

1. "ChristiaNet Poll"; http://www.marketwire.com/press-release/Christianet-Inc-703951.html.

2. Mark A. Yarhouse, "Marriage-Related Research," *Christian Counseling Today* 12, no. 1 (2004): 84.

3. "Simba Information" (Business of Consumer Book Publishing, 2009); http://www.rwanational.org/cs/the_romance_genre/romance_literature_statistics.

Chapter 5 Good Sex

1. The Barna Group, "New Marriage and Divorce Statistics Released" (31 March 2008); http://www.barna.org/barna-update/article/15-familykids/42-new-marriage-and-divorce-statistics-released.

2. Wendy Maltz and Larry Maltz, *The Porn Trap: The Essential Guide to Overcoming Problems Caused by Pornography* (New York: Harper Paperbacks, 2009).

3. Lee Wilson, "Should Married Couples Use Pornography?" Family Dynamics Institute (2005); http://www.familydynamics.net/using_pornography_porn_in_marriage.htm.

4. Quoted in Kirk Noonan, "No More Secrets," *New Man* (September/October 2005); http://www.newmanmag.com/display.php?id=11678.

5. Karen Deveny, "No Sex, Please, We're Married," *Newsweek*, June 30, 2003.

Chapter 6 A Safe Family

1. CBS News/Associated Press, "Sexting Girls Facing Porn Charge Sue D.A." (27 March 2009); http://www.cbsnews.com/stories/2009/03/27/early-show/main4896577.shtml.

2. Ceci Connolly, "Teen Pledges Barely Cut STD Rates, Study Says," *Washington Post*, 19 March 2005, A03; http://www.washingtonpost.com/wp-dyn/articles/A48509-2005Mar18.html.

3. Craig Gross and Mike Foster, *Questions You Can't Ask Your Mama about Sex* (Grand Rapids: Zondervan, 2005).

4. Sonya Thompson, "Study Shows 1 in 3 Boys Heavy Porn Users," *University of Alberta Study* (5 March 2007).

5. C. S. Lewis, *The Weight of Glory* (San Francisco: HarperOne, 2001), 33.

6. This technique is adapted from a book called *Raising Cole: Developing Life's Greatest Relationship, Embracing Life's Greatest Tragedy: A Father's*

Story (HCI, 2004) by Marc Pittman, the father of two boys, who described how he created an environment where his boys could tell him anything.

Chapter 7 A Safe Workplace

1. Anna Kuchment and Karen Springen, "The Tangled Web of Porn in the Workplace," *Newsweek*, 8 December 2008; http://www.newsweek.com/id/171279.

2. Jamie Walters, "Revving Up the 'P' Word (Productivity)," *Inc.*, 1 June 2002; http://www.inc.com/articles/2002/06/24280.html.

3. Ibid.

4. "Sex in the Workplace: Employment Law Alliance Poll Finds 24 Percent Involved in Sexually Explicit Computing," *Employment Law Alliance*, 10 February 2004; http://www.employmentlawalliance.com/en/node/1324.

5. Computer Security Institute and the Federal Bureau of Investigation; www.gocsi.com.

6. *Computerworld* 11, no. 17 (14 July 2005).

7. Walter Stern, "Pornography in the Workplace," *Savannah Morning News*, 22 April 2006; http://savannahnow.com/node/21369.

8. Sandra O'Connell, "Avoid the Web of Deceit, Porn and Litigation," *Sunday Times*, 25 September 2005; http://business.timesonline.co.uk/tol/business/article570224.ece.

Chapter 8 Seeking Help

1. J. Hampton Keathley III, "Mark 16: Accountability"; http://www.bible.org/page.php?page_id=459.

2. Matthew Paulson, "X3 Watch: Keeping the Pornography Away," *Associated Content*, 4 December 2006; http://www.associatedcontent.com/article/91724/x3_watch_keeping_the_pornography_away_pg2.html?cat=15.

Resources

Online

www.XXXchurch.com

www.x3pure.com (30 days to purity workshop)

www.everymansbattle.com

www.purelifeministries.org

www.higher-calling.com

www.sash.net (Society for the Advancement of Sexual Health)

www.slaafws.org (Sex and Love Addicts Anonymous)

www.sexhelp.com (Dr. Patrick Carnes' Sexual Addiction Resources)

Books

Recovery

Arterburn, Stephen. *Every Man's Battle: Winning the War on Sexual Temptation One Victory at a Time.* Colorado Springs: WaterBrook Press, 2000.

Black, Claudia, PhD. *It Will Never Happen to Me: Growing Up with Addiction as Youngsters, Adolescents, Adults.* Center City, MN: Hazelden, 2001.

Carnes, Patrick, PhD. *Facing the Shadow: Starting Sexual and Relationship Recovery,* 2nd ed. Carefree, AZ: Gentle Path Press, 2008.

Carnes, Patrick, Debra Laaser, and Mark Laaser. *Open Hearts: Renewing Relationships with Recovery, Romance and Reality.* Carefree, AZ: Gentle Path Press, 1999.

Earle, Ralph H., and Mark R. Laaser. *The Pornography Trap: Setting Pastors and Laypersons Free from Sexual Addiction.* Kansas City: Beacon Hill Press, 2002.

Gallagher, Steve. *Out of the Depths of Sexual Sin.* Dry Ridge, KY: Pure Life Ministries, 2003.

Maltz, Wendy, and Larry Maltz. *The Porn Trap: The Essential Guide to Overcoming Problems Caused by Pornography.* New York: Harper Collins, 2008.

Schnarch, David. *Intimacy and Desire.* New York: Beaufort Books, 2009.

Faith

Answers in the Heart: Daily Meditations for Men and Women Recovering from Sex Addiction. Center City, MN: Hazelden, 1989.

Gross, Craig. *Dirty Little Secret.* Grand Rapids: Zondervan, 2006.

Hope and Recovery: The Twelve-Step Guide for Healing from Compulsive Sexual Behavior. Center City, MN: Hazelden, 1994.

Nouwen, Henri. *Reaching Out: The Three Movements of the Spiritual Life.* Garden City, NY: Doubleday, 1986.

———. *The Return of the Prodigal Son: A Story of Homecoming.* New York: Doubleday, 1986.

Palmer, Parker J. *A Hidden Wholeness: The Journey toward an Undivided Life*. San Francisco: John Wiley and Sons, 2004.

———. *Let Your Life Speak: Listening for the Voice of Vocation*. San Francisco: John Wiley and Sons, 1999.

Software

Accountability Software: X3watch, www.x3watch.com

Internet Filtering Software: Safe Eyes, www.x3watch.com

Recovery Groups

Celebrate Recovery, www.celebraterecovery.com

LIFE Ministries, www.freedomeveryday.org

Sexaholics Anonymous, www.sa.org

Sex Addicts Anonymous, www.saa-recovery.org

Live-in Programs/Weekend Workshops

Pure Life Ministries, www.purelifeministries.org

Every Man's Battle, www.everymansbattle.com

Serenity Prayer

God, grant me the Serenity
To accept the things I cannot change . . .
Courage to change the things I can,
And Wisdom to know the difference.

Living one day at a time,
Enjoying one moment at a time,
Accepting hardship as the pathway to peace.
Taking, as He did, this sinful world as it is,
Not as I would have it.
Trusting that He will make all things right
if I surrender to His will.
That I may be reasonably happy in this life,
And supremely happy with Him forever in the next.
Amen.

—Reinhold Niebuhr

Acknowledgments

Thanks to the whole Fireproof Ministries team.

Special thanks to:

Michelle, for all that you do for this ministry.

Laura, for your support and prayers for people.

Brian, aka Info, for your willingness to serve and respond to so many people.

Hibbits, for your insights and edits and amazing work.

Miss Shellie, for your voice.

Donny, your life change inspires me.

Supan, Shatto, Jake, Richey, the Luffs, Bernie, Driscoll, and Cotter, for your wisdom and support on the board of directors.

Jharp, for your years of unwaivering support of me and the ministry and for your incredible research and writings.

All our volunteers and bloggers—this ministry could not be what it is without you all.

Craig Gross founded Fireproof Ministries and XXXchurch. com and is the author of several books, including *The Dirty Little Secret: Uncovering the Truth Behind Porn*; *Questions You Can't Ask Your Mama about Sex*; and *Starving Jesus*; and co-author of *Jesus Loves You This I Know*. Craig recently started The Strip Church in Las Vegas. He currently lives there with his wife, Jeanette, and two kids, Nolan and Elise.

www.XXXchurch.com
www.craiggross.com

Jason Harper founded the Extra Mile, an organization committed to advocating for better education and health care for inner-city children. Jason is the director of community outreach for Capital Christian Center. He is co-author of *Jesus Loves You This I Know*. He currently lives near Sacramento with his wife, Lynette, and two kids, Madison and Josiah.

www.extramilerun.com
www.jasonharper.cc

Issues of sexual addiction, sexual temptation, and pornography are real and may be affecting someone you know.

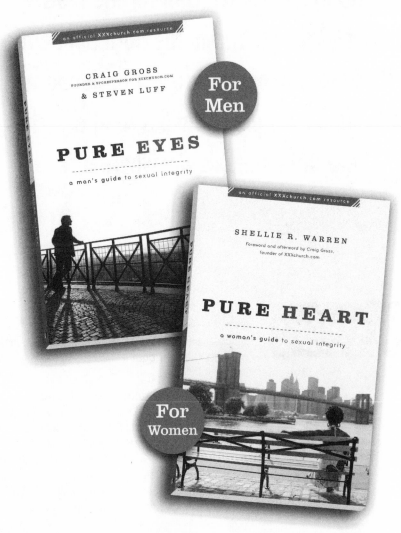

These open, honest, and biblically based guides help readers, both men and women, overcome sexual sin or remain sexually pure.

Go to XXXchurch.com for the tools you need to respond to the porn pandemic. These resources, specifically designed for individuals, couples, families, and churches, are not available anywhere else.

This website is updated daily with helps and resources for parents, women, men, youth, spouses, pastors, and more. Join the discussion! **www.xxxchurch.com**

Free accountability software available from XXXchurch or with purchase of *Eyes of Integrity*. This software automatically emails a selected accountability partner whenever a questionable internet site has been accessed. This information is meant to encourage open and honest conversation between friends and help us all be more accountable. **www.x3watch.com**

Offers 30-day online workshops featuring Steven Luff and Shellie R. Warren. These frank and open discussions are excellent companions to *Pure Eyes* and *Pure Heart*. **www.x3pure.com**

Discover the amazing love Jesus has for you.

No matter who you are, what you've done, or where you're going, Jesus loves you with a fierce and undiluted love. And he calls you to love others in the same way.

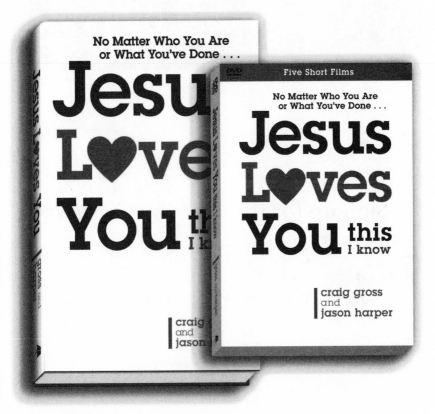

"The story of Jesus' love never gets old, and in these stories it is even newer and more beautiful and transforming than ever."—Shauna Niequist, author of *Cold Tangerines*

Don't miss the Jesus Loves You DVD and website!
www.jesuslovesyou.net